# Hitler's War
# Against
# The Jews

# HITLER'S WAR AGAINST THE JEWS

## By David A. Altshuler

A Young Reader's Version of
The War Against the Jews
1933-1945
By Lucy S. Dawidowicz

BEHRMAN HOUSE, INC.
PUBLISHERS
NEW YORK

**Library of Congress Cataloging in Publication Data**
Altshuler, David A.
  Hitler's war against the Jews.
  "Lucy Dawidowicz's research, culminating in
The War Against the Jews, 1933-1945 and A
Holocaust Reader, is the foundation of the present
narrative."
  Includes index.
  SUMMARY: Discusses the growth of anti-Semitism
in Germany from the sixteenth century until the
Holocaust during the twentieth century. Includes
topics for discussion.
  1. Holocaust, Jewish (1939-1945)—Juvenile
literature. [1. Holocaust, Jewish (1939-1945)]
I. Dawidowicz, Lucy S. The war against the Jews,
1933-1945. II. A Holocaust reader. III. Title.
D810.J4A475    940'.53'1503924    78-5418
ISBN 0-87441-222-6

Book design by Ed Schneider

10  9  8  7  6  5  4

MEIN KAMPF translated by Ralph Manheim
Copyright 1943 by Houghton Mifflin Company
Copyright © renewed 1971 by Houghton Mifflin Company
British Commonwealth, Hutchinson Publishing Group Ltd.
Excerpts reprinted by permission of the publishers

**Photographs Courtesy of:** Archives of the Leo Baeck Institute, New York, photographs by Eric
Pollitzer: pages 11, 17, 21, 25, 29, 30, 33, 35, 41, 42, 45, 62, 81, 94, 95, 101, 105, 106, 151, 171, 173,
175; Centre de Documentation Juive Contemporaire, Paris: page 57; Israel Office of Information: page
109; Landesbildstelle Berlin: pages 60, 61; The Library of Congress, Washington, D. C.: pages 2, 3, 7,
15, 23, 29, 39, 49, 51, 53, 65, 70; The National Archives, Washington, D.C.: pages 41, 73, 74, 77, 98,
101, 164, 177; Wide World Photos: pages 5, 8, 67; YIVO Institute for Jewish Research, New York: pages
69, 113, 121, 127, 129, 131, 135, 139, 140, 143, 144, 148, 153, 157, 163, 167; Zionist Archives: page
41. Cover photograph by Mike Mitchell.

For my grandparents, Morris and Anna Altshuler and Samuel and Pauline Falk

and for my rabbi, Abraham J. Feldman—

my links to European Judaism.

May their memory be for blessing.

# CONTENTS

## Part Two: The Holocaust

# ACKNOWLEDGMENTS

Lucy S. Dawidowicz's research, culminating in *The War Against the Jews 1933–1945* and *A Holocaust Reader,* is the foundation of the present narrative. I hope that this retelling will prove a worthy addition to her arduous labors.

Seymour Rossel and Jacob Behrman have guided and supported this endeavor from its inception. I am grateful that they have asked me to participate in what we all regard as an important venture for Jewish and general education.

Barbara Lettes, of the George Washington University Department of Religion, devotedly typed and retyped the manuscript, and her questions and comments were apt and helpful.

Ed Schneider, of Centrum Corporation, designed this book with his customary care and attention to detail. His aesthetic judgment and sensitivity to the text proved invaluable.

Linda Altshuler, my wife, served skillfully, not only as photo editor, but as first counselor as the text took shape.

My own contribution has been to interpret the Holocaust using skills and information acquired in my studies of the history of Judaism, particularly its development in biblical and rabbinic times. It is always a pleasure to thank my teachers, Jacob Neusner and Ellis Rivkin; their work continues to nurture my own.

David Altshuler
*Erev Hanukkah* 5738
Washington, D.C.

# INTRODUCTION

In five short years, between 1941 and 1945, the German state led by Adolf Hitler murdered six million Jews in Europe. Ever since that terrible time, people all over the world have struggled to understand: how could it have happened? How could a modern state destroy innocent men, women, and children just because they were Jews? How could so many people allow themselves to be killed? How could the modern world let this mass murder take place?

These questions have no easy answers. World War II tore Europe apart and left deep scars on those who survived it. Over thirty-five million people were killed, more than in any previous war. Two thirds of all the Jews in Europe died. These are facts. History will always remember them, but never fully understand them.

This book is about Hitler's war against the Jews. Part One, "The Final Solution," tells the story of the Germans. What made it possible for anti-Semitism to thrive in Germany, and how did this vicious ideology become the basis for a political reality and a human tragedy? To understand, it is necessary to study the life and thought of Adolf Hitler, the history of German Jew-hatred, and the actions of the German state in first persecuting and then destroying masses of innocent Jews. Many European nations have harbored anti-Semitism in modern times. There was much talk about the "Jewish question," that is, how Jews could "fit" in modern society. And many European anti-Semites argued that Jews could gain equality with Christians only by giving up much or all of their Judaism and their Jewish cultural identity. But only Hitler's Germany created what they believed to be "the *Final* Solution of the Jewish Question."

Part Two of the book is called "The Holocaust" because that is the name that Jews have given to the destruction of European Jewry. The word holocaust means "burnt sacrifice." For the Jews, it is as if millions of innocent Isaacs were actually sacrificed on an altar built by anti-Semitism. Part Two describes the tragic struggle of the Jews of Europe, how they worked together and tried to give strength to one another, and what finally was their terrible fate.

At the end of each chapter there is a section called "Issues and Values." The Holocaust was an important, world-shaking event, not only for the Jews but for humanity as a whole. The life of each one of us has been affected by it deeply. The problems which it poses, the effects it has on the decisions we make today, and the meaning it has for us as moral beings require serious consideration. The "Issues and Values" sections compare the Holocaust with other times in the history of the Jews and contrast the ideas, beliefs, and actions of the Germans with the sacred texts which make up the Judaic tradition. From biblical times until the present, Jews and Judaism have been dedicated to ethical ideals which stand against cruelty and immorality. Perhaps by gaining an understanding of the horrors of the Holocaust and how they came to be, we will better appreciate the traditional values of Judaism: righteousness and holiness, justice, and the supreme importance of human life.

Recounting the Final Solution and the Holocaust is not a pleasant task, but it is an important one. Hitler, and those he led, committed the sin of murder—yet the world did not stop them. It is our duty to learn from this terrible event, so that it may never happen again.

**Europe Under German Rule,
December 1942**

FINLAND

Helsinki

Leningrad

ESTONIA

Riga

LATVIA

HUANL

no

Vilna

Minsk

WHITE
RUSSIA

saw

ERAL
RNEMENT

ow

Lwów

UKRAINE

Kiev

TRANSNISTRIA

ARY

CRIMEA

RUMANIA

Bucharest

BLACK SEA

Sofia

BULGARIA

Istanbul

Ankara

EECE

TURKEY

Athens

CRETE

CYPRUS

EA

Allies

The German Reich

Areas under German administration

Areas under German occupation

German satellites

Italy and annexed areas

Moscow

Tula

SOVIET UNION

Easternmost German
penetration of Russia

Kharkov

Stalingrad

Rostov

Grozny

CASPIAN SEA

NETHERLANDS
105,000
140,000

PROTECTORATE
OF BOHEMIA
AND MORAVIA
80,000
90,000

BELGIUM
40,000
65,000

GERMANY/
AUSTRIA
210,000
240,000

SLOVAKIA
75,000
90,000

FRANCE
90,000
350,000

HUNGARY
450,000
650,000

YUGOSLAVIA
26,000
43,000

ITALY
8,000
40,000

# Destruction of the European Jews

Top number indicates the number of Jews
annihilated in designated areas.

Bottom number indicates the prewar
Jewish population for designated areas.

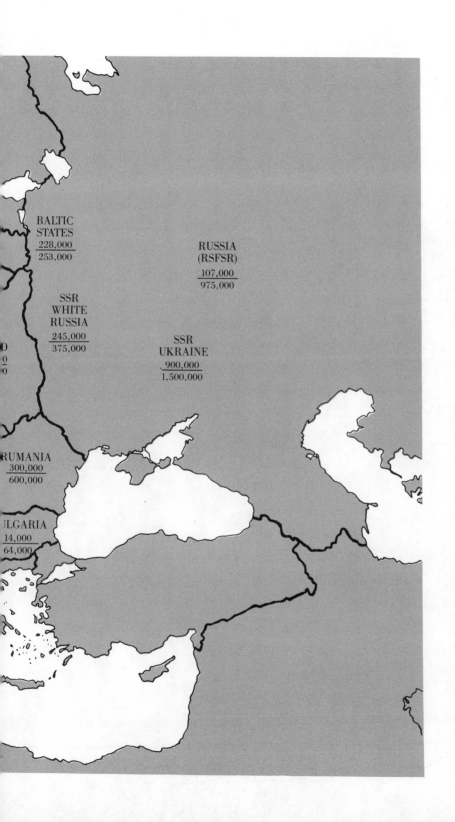

BALTIC
STATES
228,000
253,000

RUSSIA
(RSFSR)
107,000
975,000

SSR
WHITE
RUSSIA
245,000
375,000

SSR
UKRAINE
900,000
1,500,000

D
0
0

RUMANIA
300,000
600,000

ULGARIA
14,000
64,000

# PART ONE

# THE FINAL SOLUTION

Nazi high
command at a
mass rally in
Nuremberg.

# ADOLF HITLER

Adolf Hitler was not the first anti-Semite in modern times to think or talk about mass murder of the Jews. Other Jew-haters before him spoke of destroying the Jewish people, but they always ended up settling for less—keeping Jews out of certain jobs, or schools, or neighborhoods. Hitler alone succeeded in turning his vicious dreams into monstrous reality.

Only Hitler's followers took his murderous ideas about the Jews seriously. His opponents considered him crazy, and they did not see any reason to bother debating his wild ideas. Perhaps they underestimated both Hitler and his plans. He was odd-looking, of medium height, with beady eyes and a comic moustache. His hair was never neat and his face was dull and homely. He was extremely self-confident, but many thought he looked and acted like a madman.

Looking at this strange, small man, Hitler's enemies found it difficult to take him seriously. One man recalled seeing Hitler without a bodyguard in an almost empty restaurant in 1932. He could easily have shot Hitler, and years later deeply regretted that he did not. Who could have guessed, in 1932, the years of suffering and death that Hitler would later cause? In the restaurant, he looked like "a character out of a comic strip." No one would bother to shoot him then.

How did this man, with his clown's moustache and his ugly nose, come to command an entire nation? Was it his voice, which sounded with the power, firmness, and fury of thunder? Did the physical strength of his voice hypnotize them? Or did he succeed

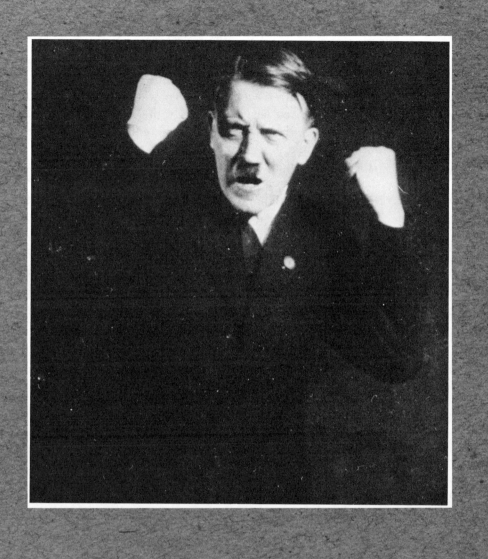

because of his message, the false and immoral claim that Jews belonged to an "inferior race"? Responsible people thought that Hitler's ideas about the Jews were only spoken to make him more popular. They believed that Jew-hatred was the way to power, a political slogan meant to appeal to the masses. But exactly the reverse was true. Hitler's hatred of Jews and his racist theories were the real reasons he wanted power. He wanted to wipe out the Jewish people.

Hitler's ideas about the Jews were at the center of his view of life. They shaped his political ambitions, and they became the most important beliefs of his National Socialist party. Out of Hitler's mind came the German dictatorship, its anti-Jewish policies from 1933 to 1945, and the murder of the Jews in Europe during World War II. Hitler's ideas were false, immoral, and insane. But we must study those ideas, because they caused such terrible destruction.

---

## HITLER'S EARLY YEARS

Adolf Hitler was born April 20, 1889, in a small Austrian town at the border of Germany. Adolf was the fourth child of Alois Hitler (1837–1903) and his third wife, Klara, who was twenty-three years younger than Alois. Adolf Hitler was never certain who or what his grandfather was. It may be that he was troubled by the rumor that his father's father was Jewish; and the rumor was well-known. One German officer was still repeating it even after World War II was over. Since Hitler condemned to death anyone suspected of being even part-Jewish, his uncertainty about his own family must surely have bothered him.

Adolf's father was an Austrian customs official, and the family moved whenever his assignments were changed. In 1894, when Adolf was five years old, they moved to a suburb of Linz, where they finally stayed. Alois retired the next year and spent his time buying and selling farms, strolling about the neighborhood, and socializing at the local tavern. His relations with his son Adolf were stormy and tense. Adolf was a lazy and uninterested student, but his father wanted him to study science and business. Adolf disliked these subjects and hoped to become a painter, an artist. Alois died in 1903, and one year later Adolf was transferred to a boarding school because of his poor grades. He left his new school a year later without taking the final examinations, and he never received a diploma. The only two subjects in which he excelled were drawing and gymnastics. His teachers later remembered Adolf as undisciplined and ill-tempered. When he left

Crowd of admirers reach out to touch Hitler, Buckelburg, 1935.

school he seemed uninterested in settling down or looking for work. He was satisfied to be supported by his widowed mother.

Hitler later wrote that his family, friends, and home town had little influence on his life. He said he did not remember hearing the word "Jew" during his father's lifetime. And the few Jews of Linz, Adolf said, he regarded merely as Germans of a different religion. He claimed that he "did not so much as suspect the existence of an organized opposition to the Jews."

But August Kubizek, Hitler's boyhood friend, remembered otherwise. Adolf Hitler, he said, was a supporter of Georg von Schönerer, an anti-Semitic politician. And several of Adolf's schoolteachers openly held anti-Semitic views. According to Kubizek, Adolf Hitler himself was a confirmed anti-Semite as early as 1904. Just fifteen years old, Hitler had begun to read the local anti-Semitic newspaper and to attend the local theatre to hear the music of Richard Wagner, a composer noted for his anti-Semitic ideas. Later, Hitler would compare Wagner with King Frederick the Great and theologian

7

**To give the German people a feeling of power, Hitler and his Nazi followers staged grandiose mass rallies.**

Martin Luther: "Whoever wants to understand National Socialist Germany must know Wagner."

THE VIENNA YEARS

Hitler's ambition to become an artist caused him to travel to Vienna in 1906. Living on money sent by his mother, he tried to be admitted to the Academy of Fine Arts. The drawings he submitted in October 1907 were rejected as unsatisfactory, and when he reapplied to the academy one year later, he was not even allowed to take the entrance test. Meanwhile his mother became ill with cancer, and she died in December 1908. Hitler went home for the funeral, and a few weeks later he returned to Vienna, where he would spend the next four years.

Very little is known about this period of Hitler's life. He quickly spent his small inheritance and his orphan's pension, then moved into a cheap boarding house. His only income came from painting scenes of Vienna on postcards, and he later described these years in Vienna as the unhappiest time of his life.

However, Vienna was an important influence on Hitler's way of thinking. The city at this time was a hotbed of anti-Semitic politics, organizations, writing, and propaganda. Despite Hitler's down-and-out way of life, he was well aware of Vienna's anti-Semitic doings. For example, he bought and read several anti-Semitic newspapers and pamphlets. He probably sampled many different writings, but we know for certain that one of his favorite writers was the racist Lanz von Liebenfels.

Between 1907 and 1910 Lanz published a series of pamphlets called "Newsletters of the Blond Champions of Man's Rights." Hitler regularly bought copies of this series, which described history as a constant battle between blond Aryan heroes and dark, hairy ape-men. Sometimes Lanz identified the ape-men as Jews, and he wrote that pogroms would soon come. Lanz advocated the swastika as an ideal symbol of racial purity, and in 1907 he hoisted a flag with the swastika over his castle. Lanz wrote that the Jews were "inferior" and a "threat" to society, and these writings influenced young Hitler even to the point of making him fear that "diseased, filthy Jews" would steal innocent young Aryan girls and abuse them.

Besides writers like Lanz, several anti-Semitic politicians greatly attracted Hitler during his years in Vienna. Georg von Schö-nerer led a Pan-German movement, and believed that new warrior heroes would unite all Germans against "primitive" ideas like Christianity and Judaism. Karl Lueger, on the other hand, founded the Christian Social party in the hope that anti-Semitism would be an easy way to win votes. Indeed, Lueger proved several times the most popular candidate in mayoral elections in Vienna. While Hitler probably did not join either of these movements, he did take many theories and political tactics from them. He did not agree with Lueger about the value of Christianity, but he did accept the picture of the Jew as unclean, unhealthy, and unpatriotic. In all, he concluded: "The Jew was no German."

---

In May 1913, Hitler left Vienna and came to Munich, a city full of people who agreed with him. Just twenty-four years old, a rootless young man without friends, without family, without work, Hitler arrived in Munich seeking himself and his destiny. At first, he lived much as he had in Vienna—peddling drawings, reading anti-Semitic papers and pamphlets, "observing" the city life. But he also began a new practice, speaking publicly to beer drinkers in taverns. The once lonely and withdrawn Hitler had a new aggressive confidence and a new self-image. He saw himself as a prophet who would help save the German nation.

In Munich there were several political parties Hitler might have joined. Throughout the city were little bands of people dedicated to struggling against the "secret Jewish conspiracy," to raising the swastika as a symbol of German racial superiority. But several years later no one could remember Hitler's belonging to any group; he was still very much a loner.

Then, in the summer of 1914, World War I broke out. Hitler stood with thousands in Munich to listen to the declaration of war, wave flags, and sing anthems. Two days later he enlisted in the army, thrilled to fight for Germany. Though nearly blinded once and wounded several times, Hitler kept returning from military hospitals to the battle front in France. He received two Iron Crosses for acts of bravery. But at the war's end, Hitler was again in a hospital bed, Germany was defeated and demoralized, and the monarchy was overthrown and replaced by the Weimar Republic. Hitler concluded that all of these problems which plagued Germany were the work of the Jews.

It was then that Hitler decided to enter politics. He returned to Munich, where he got his first real job as an educational officer in the Press and Propaganda Office of the army. His responsibilities included reporting on various radical groups in the Munich area. In 1919, Hitler joined one of those groups, the newly formed German Workers' party. The next year its name was changed to the National Socialist German Workers' party, when the new twenty-five point program that Hitler had drafted was adopted.

These years in Munich after the war were important ones in Hitler's development. He was no longer a loner, but was very much in contact with people who shared his racist views and his paranoid belief that the Jews had sabotaged the German war effort. In Munich, Hitler met Rudolf Hess, who would become his most slavish follower. He also came to know and revere Dietrich Eckart (1868–1923), an alcoholic and drug addict who blamed Jews for his own unsuccessful career as a playwright.

Eckart, who published various anti-Semitic pamphlets, be-

This picture was taken by Heinrich Hoffmann, Hitler's official photographer, at an informal meeting.

came Hitler's teacher and introduced him to many influential and wealthy racist nationalists. The most important of these was Alfred Rosenberg, a Russian émigré who brought with him the slogan, "Beat the Jews and save Russia." Rosenberg showed Hitler how to think beyond Germany. Like many Russian émigrés, Rosenberg brought to Germany a copy of the *Protocols of the Elders of Zion.* This booklet claimed to disclose the plans of a secret international Jewish conspiracy to take over the world. A pure piece of fiction, the booklet was used from the late nineteenth century on to support many long-standing lies of Jew-haters. The *Protocols* were first published in German in 1920 and then printed many times. Rosenberg wrote anti-Semitic articles and pamphlets commenting on the *Protocols,* as well as on the ideas of nationalism, race, and the rise and fall of civilizations.

From the writings of Rosenberg, Hitler saw the Jews as masterminds of the Bolshevik Revolution in Russia. Hitler went beyond this idea, to conclude that the "Jewish conspiracy" was much larger. The "facts," he believed, were that Jews were a racial group who single-mindedly pursued money and power; that Jews dominate, falsify, and exploit the press; and that "the effect of Jewry will be racial tuberculosis of nations." In speeches in 1919 and 1920, Hitler made clear that pogroms would not be enough of an answer. "We will carry on the struggle until the last Jew is removed from the German Reich."

All his life Hitler was seized by fear and hatred of the Jews. Even after he had murdered millions of them, on the very day of his own death, he wrote to the German people:

*Above all I charge the leaders of the nation and those under them to scrupulous observance of the laws of race and to merciless opposition to the universal poisoner of all peoples, international Jewry.*

ISSUES AND VALUES

**The Myth of the Jewish Race** The world's population is made up of a wide range of differing peoples. Although human beings are basically alike, distinctions such as color, shape of facial features, customs, and ideas separate us into many groups. Some of these distinctions are inherited. You are more likely to have red hair if one of your parents does; if your parents like sports, some of their influence may well "rub off" on you. Racist theories, however, take these ideas of heredity to an illogical extreme. Thus, Hitler believed so-called "scientists" who argued that the Jews were a "race" and that all Jews had similar physical characteristics which they inherited from their ancestors. These "scientists" even argued that Jews had "bad blood" and that they could never be "normal." Racists argued that character and personality are transmitted biologically, as are physical traits; Jews, they claimed, can never escape the "weaknesses" of their "race."

In fact, Jews are not a racial group but a religious and cultural one. Over the centuries many persons not originally born to Jewish parents have become Jews by conversion to Judaism. There are Indian Jews and Chinese Jews and black Jews. Indeed, Jews are much better understood as a nation, because they agree to certain standards by which to live, or as a people, because they share an attachment to the Hebrew language and the Land of Israel.

The Mishnah, trying to show that the commonalities of all peoples are more important than their differences, points out that God began His creation with only one person, Adam, to show that all people come from one family (Sanhedrin 4:5).

**Mental Illness** Ever since ancient times, people have struggled to explain very evil behavior. Some evil acts are the deliberate results of feelings such as anger or greed, while others come from unintentional mistakes or simply bad judgment. But as early as the Bible, Jews have recognized that some wrongdoing is best understood as unhealthy; that is, as stemming from mental illness. King Saul, for example, was plagued by fits during which he even attempted to commit murder. Modern psychologists suggest that mental illness may be caused by physical ailments, family upbringing, or social conditions.

The Talmud, like later Jewish and non-Jewish law, holds that mentally ill people should not be responsible for acts committed during periods of insanity, when they are not in full control of their senses. At the same time, the acts themselves are evil and must be stopped. With good reason, it has been argued that Hitler was insane. He was gripped by paranoia (unreasonable fear) and had delusions (unreal visions) about himself, Germany, and the world. In a larger sense, one might question whether mental illness might be "communicated" to others just as diseases are. A real understanding of Hitler's magnetic power over the German people may well rely on such an explanation.

CHAPTER TWO

# MEIN KAMPF

(Facing page) In 1924, Franz Eher Press announced the publication of *Mein Kampf.* They called it, "The four-and-a-half year struggle against lies, stupidity and cowardice: A settlement of accounts by Adolf Hitler."

Reading Hitler's book, *Mein Kampf,* provides much of our knowledge about Hitler and his ideas. He wrote it in 1923 and 1924, while he was in prison for organizing an unsuccessful attempt to overthrow the German government. Although *Mein Kampf* is disorganized and in places difficult to understand, its main point is clear. Hitler portrays himself, at age thirty-five, as a great intellectual and political figure. His single purpose is to write about his own greatness. Often he does not mention others who might have influenced him, and frequently we wonder about the truth of his descriptions of his early life. Yet *Mein Kampf,* plus bits and pieces added by his friends and enemies, tell us all we know about the development of Hitler's self-image and goals.

Hitler tells us very little about Linz in *Mein Kampf.* He wants to minimize the influence the town and his parents had on him. Instead he emphasizes Vienna, where he first was on his own. "For me this was the time of the greatest spiritual upheaval I have ever had to go through. I had ceased to be a weak-kneed cosmopolitan and became an anti-Semite." In Vienna, Hitler's racist ideas about Jews took shape.

Hitler says he came to his "philosophy" and "political view" by himself, and because of what he saw and read in Vienna. He records how he saw his first Eastern European Jews there: "Once, as I was strolling through the Inner City, I suddenly encountered an apparition in a black caftan and black hair locks. Is this a Jew? was my first thought." After a second look, Hitler asked himself: "Is this a Ger-

14

# Franz Eher Nachf. G. m. b. H.

## Deutschvölkische Verlagsbuchhandlung

Fernruf 20047 • München • Thierschstraße 15

Postscheck-Konto: Nr. 11840 München
Bank-Konto: Deutsche Hansabank A.-G.
München

Kommissionär:
Herr Robert Hoffmann, Leipzig

# 4½ Jahre Kampf
## gegen Lüge, Dummheit und Feigheit
### Eine Abrechnung von Adolf Hitler

**Leitspruch**

„Sie müssen sich ge-
genseitig wieder achten
lernen, der Arbeiter der
Stirne den Arbeiter der
Faust und umgekehrt.
Keiner von beiden be-
stünde ohne den ande-
ren. Aus ihnen her-
aus muß sich ein neuer
Mensch kristallisieren:
Der Mensch des kom-
menden Deutschen
Reiches!"            Adolf Hitler.

## Der Eher-Verlag kündigt „Mein Kampf" an. 1924
Die kürzere Fassung des endgültigen Titels ist wesentlich schlagkräftiger!

Hauptarchiv der NSDAP., München, Barer Straße 15

man?" To find an answer, he later reported, "I bought the first anti-Semitic pamphlets of my life." But these did not satisfy him. Rather, he felt he could only draw on his own study, his own experience, his own "slowly rising insights" to understand the Jews and the need to fight them.

Hitler devoted much of *Mein Kampf* to the criticism of early German anti-Semitic movements he regarded as imperfect. In order to make himself seem most important, he emphasized the weaknesses and errors of various parties in Vienna. When he agreed with them, he kept his comments brief. Hitler was especially critical of the Christian Social movement for not properly understanding the "Jewish danger" as racial rather than religious. The anti-Semitism of the Christian Socialists was a "sham" according to Hitler, because it allowed Jews an escape. "If the worst came to the worst, a splash of baptismal water could always save the business and the Jew at the same time."

---

THE RACIAL
QUESTION

Hitler assembled his own ideas about the Jews in *Mein Kampf*, which served as an autobiography, textbook, and party manual all in one. In *Mein Kampf*, he explained race as the most important principle of human life, and he tried to show that since the beginning, history was a story of the conflict between the Aryans and the Jews. "The racial question," he wrote, "gives the key not only to world history, but to all human culture." Therefore, civilizations rise and fall depending on how they take care of the "racial preservation of the nation." "In the blood alone resides the strength as well as the weakness of man," so the "resurrection of Germany" depends on "the clearest knowledge of the racial problem and hence of the Jewish problem."

The "Aryan" race was the champion of "human cultural development." By their nature and their "blood," the "Aryans" were chosen to rule the world. The whole existence of human civilization, then, depended on safeguarding the purity of the "Aryan" race.

*What we must fight for is to safeguard the existence and reproduction of our race and our people, the sustenance of our children and the purity of our blood, the freedom and independence of the fatherland, so that our people may mature for the fulfillment of the mission allotted it by the creator of the universe.*

According to Hitler, the state had only one purpose — watching over the purity of the racial community. The German people "must set race in the center of all life." They have "the task, not only of assembling and preserving the most valuable stocks of basic racial elements in this people, but slowly and surely of raising them to a dominant position."

The only obstacle for Hitler to overcome was the Jew. Hitler saw the Aryan as perfect, the Jew as totally evil. As the saying went, "Whoever knows the Jew knows the Devil." Thus, Jews were regarded not only as strange and different from Germans, but also as the worst type of human beings.

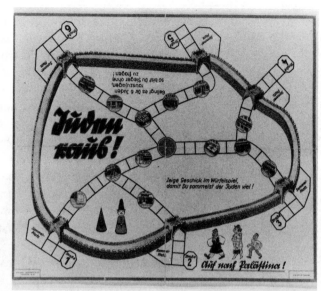

Playing board from a children's anti-Semitic game, "Jews Get Out," produced in 1938 by Fabricius Co. and sold throughout Germany in 1939 and 1940.

Hitler claimed that the "vileness" of Jews was part of their blood, that their "race" was inferior physically, mentally, and culturally. Jews, he said, "polluted" modern life with filth and disease. They "poisoned" others with germs, but somehow managed to preserve themselves. This myth that Jews carry disease goes back to the superstitions of the Middle Ages, when Jews were accused of spreading plagues and poisoning wells. Even as late as the seventeenth century, an outbreak of disease in Vienna was explained as the kind "cause by evil spirits, by Jews, by gravediggers, and by witches." Hitler believed that Jewish "poison" had defiled German family life, culture, and the press.

How had the Jews succeeded in "defiling" Germany? Hitler believed they had done so by lying, by claiming that Judaism is a religion. "Actually," according to Hitler, "they are a race — and what a race!" He believed that Jews had no language or culture of their own, that they lived off other cultures and races until they destroyed them. The Jews' ultimate goal, Hitler wrote, was to conquer the world, to achieve "domination over the nations."

**F**rom the idea of the Jew as an evil parasite, a bloodsucker contaminating the Aryan race, it was an easy step to add the notion that Jews were destroying German economic life. Hitler described Jewish business life as follows: "The spider was slowly beginning to suck the blood out of the people's pores." That image of the Jew as a selfish, greedy businessman was the one anti-Semites had used for nearly a century.

Hitler saw Jews as trying to master the world not only in business but also in labor unions, not only in the press but also in the government. As for democracy, he wrote that "only the Jew can praise an institution which is as dirty and false as he himself." Hitler viewed Marxism, which in Russia became Communism, as a Jewish movement. Marxism, too, he said, "systematically plans to hand the world over to the Jews."

Hitler's "evidence" for his theory of Jewish plans to master the world came from the history of Russia. The Bolsheviks, a party which brought violent revolution to Russia in 1918, included many Jews, most notably the leader Leon Trotsky. Hitler believed the forged *Protocols of the Elders of Zion,* and he wrote that the Jewish "conspiracy" went even further. "In Russian Bolshevism we must see the attempt undertaken by the Jews in the twentieth century to achieve world domination." All Russia, he believed, had somehow become captive of the Jews. A similar fate, he warned, faced Germany, unless it showed enough national will to resist. Hitler concluded that the Russian Empire must necessarily collapse because of this supposed "Jewish domination." His ideas of race and space, therefore, led to a foreign policy for Germany which demanded an all-out fight against Soviet Russia.

*Mein Kampf,* then, is a vision of a worldwide conflict between Aryans and Jews. It is Hitler's own plan for the triumph of "good" over "evil." He saw himself as the Messiah who would save all people from the Jews and the Devil. "Hence today I believe that I am acting in accordance with the will of the Almighty Creator: by defending myself against the Jew, I am fighting for the work of the Lord."

Hitler's image of himself was linked to his unlimited and unending fear and hatred of the Jew. "Two worlds face one another— the men of God and men of Satan! The Jew is the anti-man, the creature of another god." The title, *Mein Kampf,* means "my struggle." After Hitler wrote of his battle against the Jews, he went out to fight that battle. Before we examine how he did so, we will explore some of his predecessors.

**The Idea of Nations**   In the last two centuries, many new nations have sprung up in nearly every part of the world. Each nation asserts its right to independence and self-government, cultural development and territory. For Jews, the most important result of modern nationalism was the remarkable birth and growth of the Zionist movement, which argues that Jews have a right to the Land of Israel, to the Hebrew language, the Jewish culture and religion, as well as to freedom and statehood. But wherever they lived, Jews were also bound to their countries by love of land and language, and they always strove for equal political rights and full participation in society. Before World War II, Germany gained much from its Jewish citizens who rose to prominence as doctors, lawyers, professors, scientists, and businessmen. In return, the Jews of Germany enjoyed limited equality and most rights of citizenship.

Under Hitler, all this changed. Hitler's government regarded the Jews as foreign, and unworthy of basic human rights. Hitler accused the Jews of being a nation within a nation.

**The Risks of Democracy**   In *Mein Kampf*, Hitler argued that the German nation had to be made pure, free from all but "Aryans." His ideas of government had little to do with rule by the people, freedom for all, or equality of rights and privileges—the great values of democracy. By contrast, free choice and majority rule are at the very foundation of Judaism's view of human existence. While God is all-powerful and all-knowing, the Bible clearly states that each person, Jew or non-Jew, has the freedom and responsibility to choose between good and evil (Deuteronomy 20:19). When deciding matters of law, Jewish courts always followed the majority opinion, even when according to legend a voice from heaven sided with the minority! Of course, the Jewish sages always believed that individuals have the right to express disagreement with the majority, but the tradition held all accountable to community standards of conduct.

# THE RISE OF ANTI-SEMITISM IN MODERN GERMANY

The history of anti-Semitism in Germany began hundreds of years before Adolf Hitler. Martin Luther (1483–1546), the theologian who led the Protestant Reformation, at first hoped that the Jews would become Christians and follow him; when they did not, he lashed out against them. "Know, Christian," wrote Luther, "that next to the devil thou hast no enemy more cruel, more venomous and violent than a true Jew." Hitler later praised the violent anti-Semitism of Luther, and Luther's writings became popular as the Nazis rose to power. Thus modern German anti-Semitism in part grew out of a long history of Protestant (and, even earlier, Catholic) Jew-hatred. It was even more a result of the political development of the modern German nation.

The dawn of modern Europe proved Germany to be an essentially conservative nation, more in love with past tradition than with innovation and change. During the eighteenth century, a period known as the Enlightenment brought many new ideas to the Western world. In France and England especially, there was new interest in theories that knowledge could bring progress, and that all people might perfect themselves by following the rational laws of nature. These ideas spread to Germany, too, but most Germans were more concerned with preserving their centuries-old particular culture than adapting to new, universalistic concepts of civilization. While many Europeans were beginning to believe in human equality, most Germans clung to the idea that the German culture and spirit were superior.

Progress and enlightenment were associated not only with

**Der Stürmer**

Sonder-Nummer

 sches Wochenblatt zum Kampfe um die Wahrheit

HERAUSGEBER : JULIUS STREICHER

Preis 15 Pfennig

| Nummer 20 | Nürnberg, im Mai 1939 | 17. Jahr 1939 |

# Ritualmord

### Das größte Geheimnis des Weltjudentums

Was ist ein Ritualmord? Heute tappt auch die sogenannte gebildete Schicht in Deutschland in dieser Frage noch völlig im Dunkeln herum. Der Nationalsozialismus hat dafür gesorgt, daß es in den Köpfen aller Deutschen zu dämmern beginnt. Am gründlichsten über ihn aber ist die jüdische Bevölkerung fast aller Länder unterrichtet. In Deutschland, in Polen, in Rußland, in Rumänien, in der Türkei, in der Slowakei, kurz in all den Ländern, in denen Juden schon seit langer Zeit sitzen, ist auch das Wissen über den Ritualmord vorhanden. Die Alten erzählen es den Jungen und diese berichten es wieder ihren Kindern und Kindeskindern. Sie berichten, daß die Juden ein Mördervolk sind. Daß sie nach dem Blute der Nichtjuden gieren. Daß sie gegen alle Nichtjuden einen unmenschlichen Haß empfinden. Und daß dieser Haß besonders beim jüdischen Purimfest und beim jüdischen Osterfest (Passahfest) zum Ausbruch kommt. Zu diesen Festen ist es bei den Juden Brauch, daß sie, wo es ihnen möglich ist, Nichtjuden an sich locken, um sie umzubringen. Meist sind es beim Purimfest erwachsene Nichtjuden, die regelrecht geschlachtet werden. Zum jüdischen Osterfest aber mordet der Jude mit Vorliebe nichtjüdische Kinder. Diese mordet er in der denkbar grauenvollsten und entsetzlichsten Weise. Er knebelt und fesselt das Kind. Er quält und zerfleischt es am ganzen Körper. Er ritzt ihm die Adern. Er sammelt das Blut in Schalen. Er trinkt dieses Blut aber als verwendet es für "religiöse" Bräuche. Ein solcher Brauch wird auch am jüdischen Osterfest (Passahfest) ausgeübt. Der Jude mischt gezuckertes Blut der Nichtjuden in den Wein, den er trinkt. Und er mischt nichtjüdisches Blut in die "Mazzen" (ungesäuerte Brote), die er bäckt und zum Essen...

### Zu nebenstehendem Bild:

Im Jahre 1476 ermordeten die Juden in Regensburg sechs Knaben. Sie zapften ihnen das Blut ab und marterten sie zu Tode. Die Richter fanden in einem unterirdischen Gewölbe, das dem Juden Josfol gehörte, die Leichen der Ermordeten. Auf einem Altar stand eine mit Blut befleckte steinerne Schale.

(Bild und Bericht aus dem Buch: "Sancta Sancta", III. Band S. 174)

SEX PVERI RATISPONÆ AB IVDÆIS INTERFECTI.

## Die Juden sind unser Unglück!

the French and English, but also with the Jews. Jews had a special interest in modern ideas of universalism, because they hoped to win freedom from old anti-Jewish restrictions, and ultimately to gain political, economic, and social equality. The world-famous German-Jewish philosopher Moses Mendelssohn (1729–1786), got some important Christian support for the betterment of Jewish status. But Mendelssohn and his friends were unable to convince most Germans that "the Jew is a human being even before he is a Jew." Even some eminent scholars argued that Jews would never be loyal citizens of any state, that they would always be allies of the Devil, and that wherever Jews lived they should be treated as inferior foreigners.

Modern Germany took shape in direct opposition to the ideas of the Enlightenment which was so central to the development of France, England, and the United States. The French Revolution of 1789 popularized the belief that there are important Rights of Man which every government must protect, and fifteen years later these ideas spread through Europe with the conquering armies of the French General Napoleon. But many Germans were angered by the French military occupation of their country, and they especially hated Napoleon's idea that Jews should be given basic civic rights.

Napoleon's armies humiliated Germany in the beginning of the nineteenth century, and Napoleon made the Germans pay for peace by breaking apart their ancient Holy Roman Empire. It was this experience which prepared the way for modern Germany to emerge later on. Germans had to try to forget how the French embarrassed them militarily and politically, and they did so by thinking only about how great Germany once was, and by building toward an even more powerful Germany in the future.

---

**GERMANY TURNING INWARD**

To begin with, the Germans started seeing themselves as opposites of the French in every way. Ernst Moritz Arndt (1769–1860), who wrote poetry and political pamphlets, declared that anywhere Germans were loved, French would be hated. Since the great liberal ideas of the time—liberty, equality, fraternity—were slogans of the French Revolution, Germans began to believe that liberalism was un-German. That outlook lasted for a very long time.

The philosopher Johann Gottlieb Fichte (1762–1814) warned his defeated fellow citizens to "have character and be German." He predicted that soon enough their troubles would end.

A fifteenth century woodcut, "A warning to userers."

*Among all modern peoples it is you in whom the seed of human perfection most decidedly lies, and you who are charged with progress in human development. If you perish in this your essential nature, then there perishes together with you every hope of the whole human race for salvation from the depths of its miseries.*

Fichte was called the father of German nationalism, but also the father of modern German anti-Semitism. He argued that making Jews free German citizens would hurt the German nation. Jewish ideas were as obnoxious as French ideas. The only way he could agreed to give Jews rights, he said, would be "to cut off all their heads in one night, and to set new ones on their shoulders, which should contain not a single Jewish idea."

Similarly, Arndt believed that the Jews were internal

23

enemies of Germany as much as the French were external enemies. Jews were free citizens in Germany only because the French had forced this change; therefore, Jews did not really belong in the German nation. Arndt and his student, Friedrich Ludwig Jahn (1778–1852), gave to German nationalism the idea of "Volk," a German word which means people, but came to signify much more. "Volk" became almost a religious term, describing the innermost character of what Germans were supposed to be. For Jahn, a fiery German patriot who fought against Napoleon, "A state without Volk is nothing . . .; a Volk without a state is nothing, a bodiless airy phantom, like the Gypsies and the Jews." One hundred thirty years later, Hitler would send Gypsies and Jews to the gas chambers precisely because he did not see them as part of the German Volk.

According to Jahn, the Volk needed the state to preserve it and carry out its will. From Jahn's time until Hitler's, many Germans would believe that the state, by serving the Volk, really served God. Naturally, the Jew could only be an outsider in a "Christian" state. Even an important historian at the University of Berlin argued that Jews should not be citizens of Germany because they were a "foreign people." If the Jews want to acquire German rights, he said, they should convert to Christianity. If Jews do not become Christians, how can they be loyal to a Christian state? If they are not loyal, they can be only subjects, not citizens.

REACTIONS
AGAINST
LIBERALISM

The Jews of Western Europe gained freedom and equality in the French Revolution and its aftereffects. But Germany and other nations soon reacted against the spirit of these changes, against their French enemies, and against the idea of universal civic rights. With the defeat of Napoleon in 1815, the Germans took their revenge on the French and the Jews. Now political rights were guaranteed only for "differing parties of the Christian religion," and anti-Semitism became an important factor in the life of the German Volk. From 1815 until Hitler came to power in 1933, every attempt to improve Jewish life in Germany was followed by another attempt to keep the Jews down.

Not only did German governments take away rights they had granted the Jews, but peasants and city-dwellers demonstrated and rioted in violent pogrom attacks against Jews. Some cities even tried to banish Jews altogether. And beginning in 1819, a movement known for its new slogan of "Hep! Hep!" carried out the most violent pogroms since the Middle Ages. This movement called for "revenge" against the Jews, "who are living among us and who are increasing like locusts. . . . Our battlecry will be 'Hep! Hep! Hep! Death and destruction to all the Jews!'"

Meanwhile, Jew-hatred was developing in a new group, the early socialists. German socialists were frequently atheists, and their dislike of Christianity spilled over into disgust for Judaism as the source of the early Christian faith. In addition, socialists saw the Jews as typical of their archenemies, capitalists. In 1842, a socialist named Bruno Bauer (1809–1882) published an article on the Jewish question, where he argued against Jewish political rights. Bauer claimed that both Orthodox and Reform Judaism were worthless, and that Jews had never contributed anything to world civilization. Karl Marx, father of modern Communism, went beyond Bauer to argue that the true Jewish religion was business and greed, and that Jews saw money as their god. Marx believed that Jews would have to free themselves from this "religion" before they or anyone else could be truly free.

Despite all this opposition, Jews did gain more rights after the German Revolution in 1848, which brought a more liberal government and constitution into being. But the early gains in 1848 were more than offset by a conservative reaction which included demonstrations against Jewish rights, seizing of land by peasants, and many pogroms. New political parties and leaders spoke out against the Jews, and it became clear that no government could guarantee Jewish safety and political rights.

The title page of a children's anti-Semitic book, *The Poisonous Mushroom*, published in 1938.

**The title page of Martin Luther's *Concerning the Jews and Their Lies*, Wittenburg, 1543.**

Now writers were more openly hostile to the Jews than ever before. Paul de Lagarde (1827–1891), a professor of Bible and oriental languages, compared Jews to filthy, disgusting animals which ought to be "exterminated." That imagery was to be repeated time and again until Hitler applied it with terrifying consequences.

Various "scholars" were now constructing theories about racial differences between Aryans and Jews. Most argued that Germans needed to keep their blood as "pure" as possible, which of course meant "protecting" their "race" from any "mixing" with Jews. Such opinions were also expressed by leading figures in German cultural life. The journalist and renowned composer, Richard Wagner (1813–1883), was obsessed by a ferocious hatred of Jews, whom he saw as Germany's worst enemies.

This was the situation in which the various German states were united into a single Empire in 1871. New laws protected Jewish rights, and a liberal element in the country supported growing acceptance of Jews into various aspects of modern German life. But large segments of the population still wanted to preserve the Volk against any Jewish "intrusion." An economic crisis in 1873 was used by anti-Semites to "prove" that the Jews were trying to steal the financial life away from the country. Otto von Bismarck (1815–1898), the first Chancellor of the Empire, soon learned that it was bad politics to support liberals or Jews. That fact would remain true for most of the next sixty years, until Adolf Hitler was appointed Chancellor.

---

**Anti-Semitism** The term "Semite" comes from the name of Noah's son Shem (Genesis 10), and it is used to describe many Eastern-Mediterranean peoples who speak similar languages, including Jews, Arabs, and Assyrians. However, the modern expression "anti-

Semitism" refers to hatred of the Jews, a phenomenon with an unfortunately long history. Because Judaism, with its belief in one God, prohibition of idols, and unusual rituals, was so different from early paganism, ancient neighbors sometimes regarded the Jews as strange or "uncivilized." The growth of Christianity added a new dimension to anti-Semitism, since many early Christians believed that Jews who rejected Jesus were doomed to be abandoned by God. The Church taught that Jews were an inferior group, and to this teaching were later added the claims that Jews were unfair in their business practices, had evil political aims, and strange social behavior. All too often, tragic consequences came even from rumors or "theories" which were later proven to be outright lies. For example, claims that Jews used human blood for baking Passover *matzot* were repeated even as late as 1840 in Damascus, Syria and 1911 in Kiev, Russia. Despite the fact that these "blood accusations" were totally false, many Jews suffered violence and even death as a result of them.

**The Cause of Emancipation**   Over the past two centuries many groups, including the Jews, have enjoyed freer status and relief from certain political, economic, and social disabilities in various countries. This progress in gaining the freedom and equality we call *emancipation* began just before the French Revolution and has continued, with some setbacks, to the present day. Germany is an example of a country in which improvements were followed by enormous leaps backward. But it is not the only example. In the Soviet Union and in many Arab countries, the situation of the Jews is far worse today than at many earlier times in Jewish history. Even in the United States, Jews have had to struggle for certain basic freedoms and for equality under the law. A number of states, for example, barred Jews from public office until well into the nineteenth century. Still, the majority of the world Jewish population now lives in freedom and legal equality.

# CHAPTER FOUR

# GERMAN POLITICAL ANTI-SEMITISM, 1873-1932

**(Facing page)
Poster reading,
"Enough now:
Vote Hitler."**

Until 1873, anti-Semitism in Germany was usually the product of individual writers and public speakers, some artists and law-makers, and unorganized groups of peasants. As the nineteenth century drew to a close, though, political parties and other forms of organized political anti-Semitism began to appear. In 1878, Adolf Stöcker founded the Christian Social Workers' party in Berlin. (In Europe, the word "Christian" in the name of an organization usually showed that the organization was anti-Semitic. In fact, some Europeans even incorrectly assumed that the American YMCA must have been anti-Jewish!) Stöcker and his followers were unhappy with the government and especially with its economic policies. Small businessmen, farmers, and middle-class people in general were afraid that growing modern industry was threatening the old values of German society. Soon they concluded that the Jews must be to blame. The "Jewish conspiracy" became the single and simple explanation for whatever had gone wrong in the world.

In 1879, Stöcker made his first anti-Semitic speech: "What We Demand of Modern Jewry." He spoke, he claimed, "in the spirit of Christian love." But he declared that modern Jews were "a great danger to German national life." This was so, he said, because Jews were "most certainly a force against religion." Jews were "destructive," "anti-Christian," and did not even believe in Judaism, though they insisted on remaining Jewish. Stöcker then added the old racist claim that Jews were "a people within a people, a state within a state, a

"The Jews—Germany's Vampires," an election handbill of the German National People's Party, a right-wing party allied with the Nazis in 1932.

# Die Juden — Deutschlands Vampyre

In England zur beherrschenden Macht gelangt, haben die Juden unablässig gegen Deutschland gehetzt. König Eduard war ihr Werkzeug. Warum taten sie das? Weil Deutschland der feste Block war, welcher ihrer Weltherrschaft im Wege stand, und weil sie bei einem Weltkrieg im Trüben fischen wollten. Aus letzterem Grunde hetzten und trieben sie auch in Deutschland zum Weltkriege. Sie haben ihr Ziel erreicht: Deutschland liegt zerschmettert am Boden, 72 Milliarden sind während des Weltkrieges aus den Händen der Christen in die der Juden übergegangen. Neun Zehntel des beweglichen Kapitals, drei Viertel aller industriellen Unternehmungen sind in ihren Händen. Nur den Grundbesitz haben sie sich noch nicht so zu eigen machen können, wie sie es möchten.

## Den Vorteil vom Weltkrieg haben einzig und allein die Juden!

Haben wir darum unsere Söhne und Brüder, unsere Männer und Verlobten hingegeben? Haben wir darum vier bange lange Jahre hindurch gedarbt und gehungert?

Wahrlich nicht!

Und haben die Juden etwa die Lasten des Weltkrieges mit uns getragen? Nein! Von Beginn des Krieges an hatten sie die Lebensmittelversorgung in der Hand, sorgten für ihre Küche und für ihren Tisch, ließen die Braten in ihrer Pfanne schmoren, buken Kuchen und strichen sich die Butter fingerdick auf das Brot, während wir mit Gemüse ohne Schmalz, mit Kartoffeln und überriechender Margarine vorlieb nehmen mußten.

In die Schützengräben mochten die Juden nicht, da wäre ja ihr kostbares Leben in Gefahr gekommen. Und es gab jüdische Aerzte genug, die grundsätzlich nur Christen für k. v. erklärten. Wer in Kriegsämtern und Kriegsgesellschaften, wo man immer sein säuberlich reklamiert wurde, oder in den Etappen, wo man gut ab und krank und hinten herum „schöne Provisiönchen" in die Tasche stecken konnte, da hockten diese Leute, und wenn Germanen aus Versehen sich hineinwagten, dann dauerte es nicht lange, bis sie hinausgebissen waren. Bei den Freiwilligen, die jetzt friedliche Bürger vor Mord und Plünderung bewahren sollen, sind sie wieder nicht zu finden.

Fast ein und eine halbe Million deutscher Brüder haben ihr Leben auf dem Schlachtfelde lassen müssen. Und was ist das Ende? Lest noch einmal Hindenburgs Aufruf gegen die Flaumacherei, deren Hauptträger die Juden waren, deren Feigheit ja weltbekannt ist. Gedenkt daran, daß die total verjudete russische Botschaft in Berlin es war, die mit Hilfe des Juden Dr. Kohn das bolschewistische Gift in Deutschland einführte und dafür sorgte, daß es von zahllosen Urlaubern an die Front getragen wurde. Dort zermürbte es unser stolzes und siegreiches Heer, und der Welt bot sich das noch nie dagewesene Schauspiel, daß die Sieger in so vielen Schlachten im Heimat zurückfluten mußten, gleich als hätten sie die schwerste Niederlage erlitten. Den schmachvollen Waffenstillstand, in dem Deutschland mit gebundenen Händen dem Feind sich überlieferte und dem zweifellos ein nicht minder schmachvoller Friede folgen wird!

Wem danken wir das? Dem jüdischen Landesverrat!!!

Wer das bestreiten oder beschönigen möchte, der sei daran erinnert, daß vor wenig Tagen erst Lloyd George den Lord Northcliffe, der als Jude Stern in Frankfurt a. M. geboren wurde, öffentlich belobt hat, daß er seine Sache in Deutschland so gut gemacht hatte! Schlagendere Beweise kann es nicht geben.

Wer Ohren hat zu hören, der höre!

Wie endet die bekannte Prophezeiung aus dem Kloster Lenin, die bisher so wunderbar ihre Erfüllung gefunden hat? „Dann" — nach dem tiefen Fall Deutschlands — „wird Juda seine Hand nach der Krone ausstrecken und überall ausgerottet werden!"

Juda hat nach der Krone gegriffen, wir werden regiert von den Landsberg und Haase, von den Kohn und Davidsohn, von Levy und von Rosa Luxemburg!

Wahrlich, deutsches Volk, du hast es weit gebracht!

Ohne kriegstüchtiges Heer und Flotte, ohne Waffen gegen feindlichen Uebermut und im Innern regiert von den schlimmsten Vampyren, die du je gehabt hast.

Machtlos, wehrlos, ehrlos!

Und von denen, die das vollbracht, die dich in tiefste Schmach und Erniedrigung gestürzt, von denen solltest du weiter dich regieren, dich am Narrenseil herumführen lassen?

Nein, nie und nimmer!

Wache auf, deutsches Volk, und treibe hinaus aus den Sitzen der Regierung die, welche sie schänden!

Darum dürfen kein deutscher Mann und keine deutsche Frau ihre Stimme den Kandidaten der deutschen demokratischen Volkspartei geben, der Judenpartei, die mit jüdischem Kapital begründet ist und unter Leitung des Juden Theodor Wolff vom Berl. Tageblatt steht!

Wenn Deutschland sich wieder erholen soll von den furchtbar schweren Wunden, die der ungeheure Frevel des jüdischen Landesverrats ihm geschlagen hat, so kann dies nur geschehen durch seinen Wiederaufbau auf nationaler Grundlage. Eine einzige Partei aber gibt es nur, welche diesen Aufbau auf nationaler Grundlage uns sichert;

## das ist die deutschnationale Volkspartei!

Darum fordern wir alle unsere Mitglieder und alle unsere Gesinnungsgenossen in Nord und Süd, in Ost und West auf:

### Wählt keine andere Abgeordneten, als solche der Deutschnationalen Volkspartei!

Deutscher Volksbund,
Berlin-Schöneberg, Vorbergstr. 4.

---

separate tribe within a foreign race." Germans must protect themselves from Jews, he said, through "wise legislation." The "wise" laws he proposed included: (1) reintroducing a census by religion (Stöcker thought this would prove how rich Jews were at the expense of Christians.); (2) limiting the number of Jews who could be appointed judges;

(3) removing Jewish teachers from the elementary schools, while strengthening the schools' "Christian-Germanic spirit." Stöcker, like many after him, gained much popular support.

---

Eighteen eighty was a significant turning point. For some reason, that year began a period of aggressive anti-Semitism which lasted for twenty long years. It was as if the quiet little streams of prejudice in Germany all at once joined together in a massive flood of Jew-hatred, which filled the whole country. It began with a series of articles written by the famous historian Heinrich von Treitschke, a professor at the University of Berlin. "Even in circles of the most highly educated [Germans] . . .," he wrote, "there resounds as if from one mouth: The Jews are our misfortune!" This phrase was to ring down through all later German generations. Anti-Semites would claim that Treitschke had spoken "for thousands, perhaps millions of his countrymen." One later wrote that Treitschke's words "became a part of my body and soul when I was twenty years old."

In the fall of 1880 the "Anti-Semites' Petition" began to be circulated. Started by two schoolteachers and a minor nobleman, it was distributed by a newly formed anti-Semitic students' club. The petition asked the German government to "free" Germany from Jews, who were described as "foreigners" trying to "master" and "destroy" the German people. The petition proposed steps much like those advocated by Adolf Stöcker, and in addition it demanded that Jewish immigration be restricted, if not totally forbidden. When it was presented to Chancellor Bismarck in April 1881, the petition had two hundred twenty-five thousand signatures!

Jews in Germany were divided as to how they felt about these events. Berthold Auerbach, a Jewish novelist whose works had often idealized Germany nationalism, was in despair. "If I tell myself again that it is perhaps not so bad, the horrible fact remains that such coarseness, such deceit, and such hatred are still possible." But Leopold Zunz, the great reformer and historian of Judaism, took another view. He wrote to a friend: "Thus I live, unconcerned about the anti-Jewish agitating swine-eaters: their din is a childish imitation of the Crusades, no longer in style. World literature today and in the newspaper press are more powerful than all the blockheads aping the Middle Ages."

The "Anti-Semites' Petition" led to the creation of several

new political parties. One of the petition's organizers. Ernst Henrici, founded the Reich Social party. When Henrici spoke out against the Jews ("The religion of the Jews is a racial religion," he said.), the masses were aroused to anti-Semitic violence. Meetings of the party led to street brawls, window smashing, attacks on Jews, and even a riot in which the Neustettin synagogue was burned down.

Henrici's party lasted only two years, but several others continued political anti-Semitism. Various "reform unions" were created during this period. By 1885 there were 52 of these semipolitical anti-Jewish "clubs," and by 1890 the number rose to 136. Because of various personal and ideological rivalries, the anti-Semitic movement never really joined into one organization. But the reform unions did give anti-Semitism one sort of political unity.

One leader of the reform unions was Eugen Karl Dühring, a philosopher and economist who taught at the University of Berlin until 1877, when university officials who found him uncooperative forced him to retire. Like others who were unhappy, Dühring blamed his difficulties on Jewish plotting. He wrote that Germany had sold itself to Judaism, and that Jews were trying to destroy the state. Dühring believed Jews to be a "counterrace" separated from all humanity, and neither change nor even conversion could affect their basic evil nature. His ideas on economics and race were very influential among university students at this time.

One of those who learned from Dühring was Georg von Schönerer, who would later pass on his ideas to Adolf Hitler. Schönerer was another politician who learned that anti-Semitism would help him attract followers. He enlisted the support of German farmers and craftsmen by campaigning against Jews, who he claimed were too powerful in cities and big business. "The removal of Jewish influence from all sections of public life" was absolutely necessary, he argued.

Within a decade, the anti-Semitic parties had succeeded in attracting electoral strength. In 1887, a librarian named Otto Böckel was elected to the Hesse legislature, after stirring peasants with his fiery slogan: "Liberate yourselves from the Jewish middlemen!" Three years later, Böckel founded the Anti-Semitic People's party, which advocated "the repeal, by legal means, of Jewish emancipation." This time, his party won five seats in the legislature.

Nor was Böckel so unusual. A school principal named Herman Ahlwardt was elected to another town government in 1892, two years after he published *The Despairing Struggle of the Aryan Peoples with Jewry*. Ahlwardt lost his job when he was caught stealing

**Pages from Jewish book defaced by Nazi propaganda**

from the school treasury to cover his personal debts. Although a court ruled his charges against the Jews false, Ahlwardt was continually reelected on the campaign theme that he was a victim of Jewish plotting. The only chance Germans had against Jews, he said, was to "exterminate those beasts of prey." The success of this kind of campaigning led the most prestigious party in Germany, the Conservatives, to adopt anti-Semitic demands in their platform. It was now clear that fighting the "Jewish influence that decomposes our people's life" was an important tool for political power.

**T**he 1890s brought even more support and organization to the anti-Semitic movement. One reason for this development was fear aroused by the growth of the Social Democratic party, which was not anti-Semitic. In the 1890 elections, the Social Democrats amassed 1.4 million votes, most of them from industrial workers who hoped that socialism and radical change would give them a fair share of the economy. These workers did not find anti-Semitism appealing, nor did they have any romantic ideas about Germany's "glorious" past.

The middle classes, in contrast, became very nervous about the growing power of the Social Democrat workers. They wanted to preserve Germany as it was, not to make radical changes which might affect the stability of economic or political life. Thus the middle classes turned heavily toward the conservative parties, and many of those candidates were anti-Semites. In 1893, the anti-Semitic vote was four hundred thousand and over the next two decades nearly ninety anti-Semitic candidates were elected to the Reichstag. All were Protestants, and none were workers. Most were small businessmen, teachers, and professionals who had experienced economic hardships or were otherwise uncertain about the future. They shared a deep frustration, and they resented the "outside" forces which seemed to be preventing them from success. Anti-Semitism gave them a way to express their unhappiness, and the Jews became their scapegoats.

Three major middle-class organizations were founded in 1893, and all of them contributed to political anti-Semitism. In 1900, the Pan-German League, the National Germanic League of Clerks, and the Agrarian League had memberships totalling nearly one-half million, and there were also numerous smaller anti-Semitic student organizations and even sports clubs. By the turn of the century, anti-Semitism had infected Germany. One book dealer found vast quantities of anti-Semitic literature in private libraries that he bought for resale. "Every year," he wrote, "tens of thousands of anti-Semitic pamphlets are sent free to all officials of the state and members of the upper [classes]."

**T**he next cycle of anti-Semitism came with World War I. By mid-1916, the war had begun to go badly for Germany. There were no military victories—only food shortages, hardships, wounded, and dead in battle. Blaming the Jews became a way of "explaining" whatever was going wrong. Jews were accused of not

# Judenglocke

### frei nach Schiller

### Zeitgemäße Satire aus dem Judenleben

fighting for Germany, and of taking easy jobs and trying to profit from the war industry. Hitler later wrote in *Mein Kampf* what many anti-Semites grumbled during the war: ". . . In the year 1916–17 nearly the whole production was under the control of Jewish finance. . . . The spider was slowly beginning to suck the blood out of the people's pores."

The Weimar Republic, born out of the German defeat in World War I, issued a new constitution which at long last gave Jews complete political equality. The laws improved for Jews, but in the minds of vast numbers of Germans, the Jews remained an internal enemy, responsible for Germany's defeat and for its losses of monarchy, wealth, territory, and prestige. In 1920, the National Socialist German Workers' party (the Nazi party) platform declared that Jews should not be regarded as members of the German Volk or as citizens. The German National People's party took a stand "against the predominance of Jewry in government and public life."

Parliamentary democracy survived in Germany for barely over one decade, which witnessed the irresistible rise of the Nazis, the growth of over four hundred anti-Semitic societies, and the publication of as many as two hundred anti-Semitic magazines. Anti-Semitism was common in legislatures and universities, and violence often ruled the streets. By 1926, even the most law-abiding German Jews began to talk about learning how to defend themselves.

By the end of 1920, the German translation of the *Protocols of the Elders of Zion* had sold one hundred twenty thousand copies. A Jewish reporter at that time wrote:

> *In Berlin I attended several meetings which were entirely devoted to the* Protocols. *The speaker was usually a professor, a teacher, an editor, a lawyer, or someone of that kind. The audience consisted of members of the educated class, civil servants, tradesmen, former officers, ladies, above all students, students of all faculties and years of seniority. . . . Passions were whipped up to the boiling point.*

It was a world filled with hate, driven by fear. The Germans were in search of a mysterious way back to the happiness they believed was stolen from them by the Jews. In 1923, the Nazis had won eight hundred thousand votes. In 1930 they had six and one-half million. In 1932, the last free election of the Weimar Republic in Germany, fourteen million voters out of forty-five million voted for the Nazis. This was the result of one hundred fifty years of growth of anti-Semitism in Germany.

**Patterns of Discrimination**   Some German laws before and during Hitler's rule placed severe limitations on Germany's Jewish citizens. Frequently, anti-Semites would defend such laws by saying that Jews themselves discriminated against non-Jews. But an examination of the Bible shows that the Jews were more sensitive to strangers, whom they were commanded to treat fairly, since they were once strangers in the land of Egypt (Leviticus 19:33-34). The first century Jewish teacher, Hillel, advised that one should not judge another until standing in the other person's shoes (Avot 2:5); and in the broadest sense, Deuteronomy proclaimed "Justice, justice, shall you pursue (16:20)."

In the United States, "subtle" patterns of social discrimination against Jews have appeared from time to time. Until recently, for example, it was common for some colleges, business firms, hotels, and country clubs to exclude Jews or limit Jews by means of a "quota." In the Soviet Union and some Arab countries, as in Nazi Germany, anti-Jewish policies have been adapted by the government, making public and official laws out of despicable private sentiments.

**Scapegoating**   In ancient times, Jews used to send a goat out into the wilderness, believing that the sacrificed animal would carry their guilt away in the eyes of God. They called this animal a "scapegoat." More recently, when people speak of "scapegoating" they mean blaming our own troubles or our own faults on others. Many times, it has been the Jew who has been used by more powerful people as a kind of scapegoat. Jews have been blamed for whatever social, political, or economic difficulties existed in society. Jews were often seen as foreigners taking advantage of the natives, middlemen taking from the poor to become rich, and immoral influences. Hitler claimed that the Jews were responsible for the defeat of Germany in World War I and that they were frustrating Germany's struggle to return to her "glorious past." Hitler's followers found it easy to blame the Jews for the decline of Germany's prosperity, for its political and military difficulties, and for all sorts of other problems. But World War II left Germany in ruins and the German people poorer and more destitute than ever, even as the Final Solution destroyed European Jewry. In the end, hatred and violence often prove harmful to the oppressors as well as to the victims.

# CHAPTER FIVE

# THE NAZIS IN POWER: ANTI-JEWISH LEGISLATION, 1933-1935

(Facing page): "Rid of misery, rid of Jews, Vote List 1, the National Socialists." A Nazi election poster.

On January 30, 1933, Paul von Hindenburg, President of the German Republic, administered the oath of office to Adolf Hitler, whom Hindenburg had decided just the day before to make Chancellor. Hitler recited: "I will employ my strength for the welfare of the German people, protect the Constitution and laws of the German people, conscientiously discharge the duties imposed on me and conduct my affairs of office impartially and with justice to everyone." But when Hitler spoke those words, he had already laid his plans to destroy the laws he was swearing to protect. Without any sense of fairness or justice, he was about to wage a fierce war against his enemies—democracy, freedom, and above all the Jews, who represented to him everything he hated.

Hitler became Chancellor because his National Socialist party had won about one-third of the votes cast in November 1932, more than any other party. His government united various conservative parties, but Hitler hoped for more popular support, so his first official act was to call for new elections on March 5. He promised the Germans a "national awakening" and proclaimed that he would put an end to the "shameful past." On February 4, he persuaded Hindenburg to sign a decree giving the police power to prohibit public meetings, and to stop publications which might "endanger" public safety. Right away, Hitler was able to use this decree against his political opponents to hurt their chances in the upcoming election.

**H**itler came to power legally, but his intentions were to break the law. Sensible people were sure that Hitler could not last long, that decency, reason and political order would — must — reassert themselves. Could any civilized nation trade the rule of law for the rule of terror? But the Germans had now begun an era of evil which would consume the nation for twelve endless years. The frenzy of mass meetings would replace the decision in the voting booth, and terror in the streets would define the politics of the Third Reich. The Germans would live by only two principles: the rule of the Führer, Hitler; and the dominion of race.

On February 27, the Reichstag building was set on fire, and an insane Communist was found on the scene. Although the details of guilt for the fire were never uncovered, and some suspected that Hitler's party may even have put the Communist up to the plot for political reasons, Hitler took swift advantage of the situation. He issued a series of emergency decrees, supposedly to combat Communist acts of violence endangering the state, but really to limit all basic freedoms — of the press, speech, assembly, and privacy. He shocked German citizens into believing that his opponents were traitors, so the Nazis not surprisingly won a strong forty-four percent of the votes.

By now the Nazis' private army, the Storm Troops, had grown to four hundred thousand. Its only mission was to terrorize those whom Hitler hated — Communists, Socialists, trade union workers, and especially Jews. With his enemies under constant pressure of attack, Hitler was quickly taking over all the powers of the government. Nazi delegates, the conservative parties, and the Catholic Center party voted to make him dictator for four years, and gave him the right to enact laws even if they contradicted the Constitution. Later, Hitler himself would simply renew his term of office. In ten days, the Storm Troops took fifteen thousand prisoners into "protective custody." By July the National Socialist party was declared the only legal political party. Hitler announced, "The party has now become the state."

**H**is power secure, Hitler prepared to deal with the Jews. He summoned Josef Goebbels, his Minister of Public Enlightenment and Propaganda, and gave him instructions. Goebbels recorded that meeting in his diary:

(Above) Josef Goebbels, Reich Minister of Public Enlightenment and Propaganda. (Left) Jews become increasingly isolated, humiliated and terrorized. (Below, left) *Der Stürmer*, special issue, "Murderers from the beginning: Jewish World Bolshevism from Moses to the Communist International."

*We shall only be able to combat the falsehoods abroad if we get at those who originated them or at those Jews living in Germany who have thus far remained unmolested. We must, therefore, proceed to a large-scale boycott of all Jewish business in Germany. Perhaps the foreign Jews will think better of*

41

Daß das Judentum niemals wieder auch nur den geringsten Einfluß in unserem Volke erhält, dafür mußt Du durch Deine Haltung dem Juden gegenüber sorgen.

**Erkenne den wahren Feind!**

Wenn Du dieses Zeichen siehst...

Jude

**The front and back covers of a four-page anti-Semitic flyer, "When you see this symbol [the yellow star], know your true enemy," 1941.**

*the matter when their racial comrades in Germany begin to get it in the neck.*

The organization of the anti-Jewish boycott showed Hitler's "talent" for turning anti-Semitism and mob passion for pogroms into "meaningful" political action. Storm Troops and Nazi hooligans terrorized Jewish businesses, and the police stood idly by. Hermann Göring, a cabinet minister, proclaimed: "I will ruthlessly set the police at work wherever harm is being done to the German people. But I refuse to make the police the guardians of Jewish department stores." Violence by Storm Troops was defended by official propaganda: "German Jews are our hostages. We will hold on to them."

This massive series of attacks aroused world criticism, and the strongest protests were made on behalf of German Jews. There was talk, especially in the United States, of boycotting German goods. Hitler decided to defend his policies by claiming that Jews were part of a worldwide conspiracy to destroy Germany. At the same time, Göring summoned German Jewish leaders to his office and warned them to stop spreading horror stories about Hitler—"otherwise pogrom."

At first the Jews resisted these warnings, but finally they submitted to the unending threats of violence. Cables, telegrams, and letters were sent abroad, much like this one sent from Berlin to the American Jewish Committee on March 30, 1933:

> *According to newspaper reports, atrocity and boycott propaganda against Germany is continuing overseas, apparently in part also by Jewish organizations. As Germans and Jews we must enter a decisive protest against this. The dissemination of untrue reports can only bring harm, affecting the reputation of our German fatherland, endangering the relations of the German Jews and their fellow citizens. Please try urgently to see to it that every atrocity and boycott propaganda report is halted.*

(The American Jewish organizations realized that German Jews were being forced to send telegrams like this.)

The Nazis organized the boycott of Jewish businesses carefully. In one town, they even placed advertisements in the local newspaper listing Jewish individuals and stores, and explaining that these were part of "international Jewry" which had spread "atrocity propaganda" against Germany. The Nazi party issued instructions that Storm Troops should serve as "protective guards" in front of Jewish stores to "inform" the public that these were owned by Jews. Hitler announced that the boycott should last one day and that violence should be avoided, but the police were advised not to interfere, and for three full days violence against Jews was common throughout Germany. In Kiel, a mob was said to have lynched a Jewish lawyer.

Individual Jews in public life suffered just as did Jewish businesses, even when violence was restrained. Hundreds were being forced from their jobs—judges and lawyers, journalists and musicians, government workers and university professors. Throughout this period of threats and resignations, the German Department of Justice agreed to "limit the influence" of Jews in order to satisfy the "wishes of the people."

The extent of these dismissals and forced resignations upset even President Hindenburg, who up to now had cooperated unhesitatingly with Hitler's every wish. Hindenburg wrote to Hitler to protest, not out of compassion for the Jews or concern for the law, but because the discrimination had harmed some Jewish veterans of the German army. Hindenburg believed that mistreatment of veterans was dishonorable. "If they were worthy to fight and bleed for Germany," he wrote, "then they should also be considered worthy to continue serving the fatherland in their professions." Hitler replied the next day and defended his actions against harmful Jewish influences. He thanked Hindenburg for his "generous and humane" approach and "noble motives," and he assured him that "the solution of this problem will be carried out legally."

MANIPULATING
THE LAW

Indeed, Hitler was able to use the law even more effectively than violence as a weapon to eliminate Jews from government service and public life. Eventually, the Third Reich enacted some four hundred laws and decrees, which ultimately led to the destruction of European Jewry. Two days after Hitler wrote to Hindenburg, the first of these laws barred "non-Aryans" and political opponents of the Nazis from civil service. Hindenburg's objections were met by a paragraph which allowed war veterans and their relatives to remain at work. Other laws during this same month, April 1933, pushed Jews out of legal practice, university careers, and positions in the arts and the press.

To simplify this procedure, a law passed on April 11 defined exactly what was meant by "non-Aryan." A "non-Aryan" was anyone "descended from non-Aryan, especially Jewish, parents or grandparents," even if only one parent or grandparent was a "non-Aryan." From then on, government workers had to prove their lineage with documents like birth and marriage certificates, and a special "expert on racial research" was employed by the Minister of the Interior to judge "doubtful" genealogies. The Nazi definition was simple: a Jew is a Jew is a Jew—that is, down to the third generation. It did not matter if one of your grandparents converted to Protestantism and your mother married a non-Jewish military hero. The grandchild of a Jew would always be a Jew according to the "racial" definition.

Having singled the Jews out, Hitler used the remaining months of 1933 to institute new anti-Semitic laws. Kosher slaughtering of animals was forbidden. The citizenship of Jews whose families had immigrated to Germany from Eastern Europe was revoked. Farmers with any trace of Jewish blood were denied all rights of family property inheritance. These and other measures had in just a few months turned the dreams of popular anti-Semitism into reality. And Hitler had won many friends by ousting Jews from important jobs and giving those positions to loyal Nazi party supporters.

**The synagogue of Baden Baden set aflame by the Nazis, November 1938.**

Now Hitler turned to solidifying his own power. The law, the courts and judges, the police, and the press all bent to his will. All sources of opposition had been crushed or had collapsed. Protestant and Catholic clergy traded their blessings for the right to keep their religious ceremonies and institutions. Most professors and intellectuals, like most lawyers and judges, sacrificed sense and honor, submitted to the Nazi state and enhanced it with their prestige. The army, believing it would be restored to grandeur, climbed on the bandwagon.

President Hindenburg died in August 1934, and Hitler "legally" became both president and chancellor. By 1935, Hitler had succeeded in making Germany a unified and militarized vehicle of personal power. In May 1935, he assured Germany's European neighbors and the world that he wanted power only for peace. The government even drafted official statements condemning mob violence against

Jews, probably because Hitler considered terror in the streets ungovernable.

But on September 15, 1935, the most vicious anti-Jewish laws, the so-called "Nuremberg Laws" were adopted unanimously by the Reichstag. "Purity of German blood" became a legal category, and marriage between Germans and Jews was outlawed. Hitler explained in *Mein Kampf* that such marriages would be as evil as those "between man and ape." More serious still was the Reich Citizenship Law, which made race the determining factor in excluding Jews from any citizenship rights. Within a few short years, questions of race would make the difference between life and death.

During the next few years, up until 1938, no substantial anti-Jewish legislation was enacted. Instead, the SS, the most prestigious and dreaded branch of the Nazi movement, increasingly began to take full power over the Jews.

---

ISSUES AND VALUES

**The Totalitarian State** People sometimes conclude that the best form of government is to let one person rule totally. In times of emergency, even free nations sometimes give extraordinary powers to the government. Usually these powers—the power to outlaw dissent, the power to control the courts, or the power to enforce laws through extreme methods—are granted on a temporary basis, just until the emergency is passed. But in Hitler's Germany (and in Italy under Benito Mussolini and in Russia since 1917) dictatorship was seen as a permanent cure. Germany became a *totalitarian* state, a state in which the individuals were thought to be less important than the people as a whole and all were ruled by one man whose word was law. Opposition parties and criticism in the press were outlawed.

As early as biblical times, Jews believed that no individual or government should be given too much authority. Deuteronomy 17 warns that a Jewish king should abide by God's law, and the prophets of old often criticized the kings of Judah and Israel for not doing so. The Jews hoped for a time when earthly kings would not be needed at all, when, in the words of Zechariah, "the Lord shall be King over all the earth (14:9)." Rabbi Hanina said, "Pray for the welfare of the government, since but for fear of it, people would swallow each other alive (Avot 3:2)." But Rabban Gamaliel, son of Judah the Patriarch, added, "Be careful of the ruling powers, for they bring no person near to them except for their own need; they seem to be friends as long as it is to

46

their gain, but they do not stand with a person in his time of stress (Avot 2:3)."

**Using Propaganda**   Totalitarian governments often try to protect their power by controlling all information. They censor the press or force the newspapers to print what they wish to have printed, rewrite history, and even have new textbooks written to order. In this way, they try to teach their people to "agree" with the government. The First Amendment to the Constitution of the United States protects the freedom of speech and the freedom of the press. Democracy depends on the right of the people to dissent, and dissent depends on the people's ability to know what the truth is. So, too, the Bible forbids the telling of untruths about others and calls upon each of us to object when untruths are spread (Leviticus 19:16). The use of propaganda, the spreading of an "official" lie to convince people of a "truth" the government would like them to hold, sometimes is comparable to inaccurate advertising which companies do for their products or services.

# THE SS: INSTRUMENT OF THE FINAL SOLUTION

In 1936 a standard lecture of SS units contained the following passage: "The Jew is a parasite. Wherever he flourishes, the people die. . . . Elimination of the Jew from our community is to be regarded as an emergency defense measure." In *Mein Kampf*, Hitler defined gassing Jews as an "emergency defense" measure, and the SS became the central vehicle for that Final Solution of the Jewish Question.

The SS *(Schutzstaffel,* German for "Defense Corps") came into being in 1925, by Hitler's order. It was a select group of efficient, elite men drawn from the Storm Troops to serve as a completely dependable bodyguard for the Führer, the Nazi leadership, and party meetings. Although it was always highly disciplined, obedient, and loyal, the SS remained quite small and undistinguished until Heinrich Himmler was appointed its leader in 1929. Soon Himmler and the SS were Hitler's most important and powerful agents.

## HEINRICH HIMMLER

Himmler was born in 1900 to a middle-class Catholic family, and the diary he began to keep in 1914 shows that his early life was rather ordinary, even dull. He learned discipline at home and in an officer training program during World War I, became an avid nationalist with interests in politics as well as military matters. In his early twenties, he began to read giant quantities of anti-Semitic litera-

ture. In 1923, Himmler joined the Nazi Party, and in 1924 he wrote that Hitler "is a truly great man, and above all a genuine and pure one. His speeches are splendid works of Germandom and Aryanism."

Himmler quickly worked his way up the party ranks, from secretary, to assistant propaganda minister, to head of the SS. At the age of twenty-nine, he was at the top of his chosen career, the professional Nazi. His SS position allowed Himmler to combine nationalism with militarism and anti-Semitism, to spy and inform, and ultimately to murder in a disciplined, unfeeling, and cruel fashion. His rigid, fanatical ideas of duty and obedience made him one of Hitler's most loyal followers. No wonder the SS's most distinctive insignia was the death's-head.

When Himmler was appointed, the SS had only 280 members, compared with 60,000 members in its parent group, the Storm Troops. Himmler decided not only to expand his force, but to convert it into an elite, racially "pure," and especially brave and loyal unit. By the end of 1930, the SS had nearly three thousand members, and the Storm Troops had become jealous of the SS's prestige. Hitler made the SS independent of the Storm Troops, giving them black uniforms in contrast with the Storm Troops' brown shirts, and he regarded them as his most trusted force. On induction, SS men took this oath: "I swear to you, Adolf Hitler, as Führer and Chancellor of the German Reich, loyalty and valor. I pledge to you and to the superiors whom you will appoint obedience unto death, so help me God."

Himmler hoped to shape the SS from racially "superior" Germans, who would eventually produce a whole class of leaders for Germany. Candidates were checked carefully as to their ancestry, and they were not allowed to marry any woman until she was similarly investigated. Himmler encouraged SS men to have children and to settle in rural areas, which he thought would provide the best setting for raising valuable racial stock. The SS grew rapidly, from fifty thousand when the Nazis took power, to nearly a quarter of a million on the eve of the war. Within the SS, the Special Troops division was Hitler's private bodyguard, while the Death's-Head Units were assigned to patrol concentration camps.

When the Nazis came to power, so many Germans were arrested under "protective custody" that the prisons were filled to overflowing. Dachau, the first concentration camp, was one of ten such detention centers in use by the summer of 1933, with over twenty-five thousand political opponents, writers, Jews, and other "unpopular" people being held. Soon all of these camps came under Himmler's

**Nazi troops
march on display,
Munich, 1935**

command, outside the normal government and ordinary processes of
law.

Another terrorist division of the SS was its Security Service
(SD), established in 1930 to find disloyalty, treason, and foreign
agents within the Nazi party. Eventually, it gathered intelligence for
Hitler throughout Germany and all of Europe. Himmler appointed
Reinhard Heydrich to head this subdivision.

Like Himmler, Heydrich was in his teens during the war.
Already a "fanatic about pure race," he joined various Volkist, anti-
Semitic groups. Heydrich was particularly committed to anti-Semitism
because, like Hitler, he was rumored to be part-Jewish. These rumors
were untrue, but they injured his pride and honor, and he became a
furious anti-Semite as well as an uncompromising Nazi. In appearance, Heydrich was every bit an Aryan, and he was described as the
"Blond Beast" as well as a "young evil god of death." After an
unsuccessful military career, Heydrich was brought to Himmler's

attention, and he rose rapidly to power. By April 1934, Himmler and Heydrich had succeeded in gaining power over all political police functions, including the prestigious Gestapo, the Secret State Police Office. In the next two years, they were able to create with Hitler a centralized, nationalized, and Nazified police system under total SS control. Between 1929 and 1939, Himmler had built his tiny corps of 280 men into a vast network of almost 250,000 regular security, criminal, and political police. The SS now extended even beyond the borders of Nazi Germany, and soon it would become the instrument for the destruction of European Jewry.

---

STRATEGIES FOR HANDLING THE JEWISH QUESTION

**A**s the SS was growing and developing, the Jewish question was not a central concern for Himmler or Heydrich. Later, within the Security Service of the SS, the department for domestic affairs included a separate desk for Jewish affairs. The officer in charge of this desk hired Adolf Eichmann at the end of 1934 as his expert on Zionism. About a year later, they began an ambitious research program to gather information about prominent Jews in Germany and abroad. Projects focused on important organizations, Orthodox and "assimilationist" groups, the Jewish press, and the Zionist movement. At the same time, the Gestapo in Berlin established a division to investigate "enemies of the state," including Freemasons, émigrés, religious associations, and Jews.

These police and investigative offices aside, there was no clear-cut government or party policy regarding the Jewish community in the years immediately following the boycott, mob violence, and discriminatory legislation. Until as late as 1938, Jews were allowed to emigrate from Germany, and Jewish organizations were even permitted to encourage and aid such emigration. Government police did spy on the Jewish community, but the Ministry of Economy also awarded production contracts to Jewish firms, and the Foreign Office even made agreements for currency exchange with the Jewish Agency in Palestine.

In 1934 it was widely believed in Germany that the Jewish question had already been settled. But few Nazi leaders were satisfied. A single, straightforward policy was still needed. Minister of Public Enlightenment and Propaganda Goebbels suggested formal recognition of a ghettoized Jewish community. German Jews already had their own cultural association, which provided jobs for actors, singers,

musicians, and other entertainers who were now cut off from general
audiences. Goebbels believed that this sort of segregated, second-
class community model might have other uses as well. Response in the
Jewish press seemed to show cautious interest in this idea, but plans
for further formalization were disbanded, perhaps because Hitler
himself rejected them.

       The SS leadership took a stand different from that of Goeb-
bels. They wrote in 1934 that only "armchair anti-Semites" could be
satisfied with the present status of the Jews. The party, they claimed,
needed to "keep alive an awareness of the Jewish problem within the
German people." Several long-range solutions were proposed, including encouraging separatism, nationalism and even Zionism among
German Jews, in hopes that they would leave Germany permanently.
Against those organizations and leaders encouraging the Jewish people
to stay and make the best of German life, police actions were taken. On
the other hand, Heydrich wrote in 1935 that: "The activity of Zionist-
oriented youth organizations [training] . . . Jews for agriculture and
manual trades prior to their emigration to Palestine lies in the interest
of the National Socialist state's leadership." Thus the Nazis seemed to
applaud Zionism, because they believed it to be truer to Jewish
"racial" characteristics than any form of German Judaism or even

Christianity (for Jews who converted).

But, had Eichmann read *Mein Kampf* (at his trial he admitted he never had), he would have seen that Hitler made no distinction among Jews, Zionists or not. "This apparent struggle between Zionistic and liberal Jews disgusted me," Hitler wrote, "for it was false through and through, founded on lies." *Mein Kampf* also makes clear Hitler's view of Palestine as a Jewish homeland: "All they want is a central organization for their international world swindle . . . a haven for convicted scoundrels and a university for budding crooks." A government official reported in 1937 that Hitler had decided that Jews should all go to Palestine, so there would be "only *one* center of Jewish trouble in the world." At about this time a Gestapo official told a Jewish leader that it would be better if Jews went not to America but to Palestine, because "there we will catch up with you."

Meanwhile, an SS research paper was written to define the Jewish question more carefully. It stated: "The Jew already as a person is a 100 percent enemy of National Socialism, as proven by the difference in his race and nationality. Wherever he tries to transmit his work, his influence, and his world outlook to the non-Jewish world, he discharges it in hostile ideologies. . . ." Here, then, was the germ of the Nazi rationale—the Jew, simply by being a Jew, was an enemy of the Aryan, the Nazi party, and the German state. Himmler also took up this notion, seeing Jews as "subhumans," and therefore enemies of Germany. The SS, he wrote, would defend "the honor, the greatness, and the peace of the Reich. . . . Pitilessly we shall be a merciless executioner's sword . . . whether it be today, or in decades, or in centuries." Thus, at a time when Germany was already talking of war against her European neighbors, the SS was beginning preparations for an internal war against German Jewry.

---

**Following Orders**   Hitler could not have implemented his plans for the Final Solution without the help of the German people as a whole and thousands of military and government officials in particular. After the war, many Nazi leaders and party members argued that when they killed Jews they were "just following orders." At his trial in 1961, Adolf Eichmann pleaded just such a defense, saying that he would not have hesitated to send even his own father to the gas chambers had he been ordered to do so. But most legal systems hold that an individual is responsible for his or her actions, even when they are the result of someone else's command or order. The Bible commands that one not follow the majority to do evil (Exodus 23:2). And in Leviticus 19:17 it says, "You shall reprove your fellow man, and do not incur sin because of him."

**Modern Jewish Nationalism**   For nearly two thousand years Jews throughout the Diaspora dreamed of returning to rebuild their homeland in Israel. Scattered throughout the world, they prayed for the Messiah to come and lead them back to Jerusalem. Finally, in the nineteenth century, many great Jewish thinkers began to ask whether such a return needed to wait for the Messiah. Impressed by the growth of nationalism all around them, by the ability of European nations to proclaim their independence and assert their rights of sovereignty, the Jews of Europe who founded the Zionist movement argued that there should be a Jewish homeland and a state for the Jews in Palestine. At the first World Zionist Congress in 1897, Theodor Herzl urged Jews everywhere to take part in the reclamation of the Holy Land and the renewal of the Jewish people on its own soil. As the movement developed, Herzl's political platform was broadened by such leaders as Ahad Ha'am and Martin Buber who formulated ideas concerning the religious and cultural role of Israel as a "spiritual center" for all Jewry.

# FOREIGN POLICY, RACE, AND WAR

**T**he task of German foreign policy, Hitler wrote in *Mein Kampf*, was to "preserve, promote, and sustain our people for the future." Because Germany had been weakened during and since World War I, and because internal enemies had betrayed the state, the first of Hitler's goals was domestic—"to restore to the nation its strength in the form of a free power state." Next, he planned, would come war and expansion into foreign territory. Thus domestic and foreign policy served each other, and both were geared to creating the "Volkist instrument of strength."

When Hitler became dictator of Germany, *Mein Kampf* became the blueprint for German domestic and foreign policy. The only ideals of these policies were racial supremacy and the power of the Nazi state. First, Germany had to rid itself of internal enemies. "Whoever wants to act in the name of German honor today must first launch a merciless war against the internal defilers of German honor," Hitler wrote. This war, of course, would be waged especially against "the foul enemy of mankind," the "inexorable Jew." The task "is and remains a bloody one."

The second goal, of restoring German strength, required building the armed forces. From the day he took power, Hitler began, in secret, to construct a military organization to serve a racially purified Germany. Six months later, Germany withdrew from both the international disarmament conference at Geneva and the League of Nations. When, in 1935, Germany reinstituted the military draft, the

FRAUEN, MÄDCHEN
HÜTET EUCH VOR
DEM SCHÄNDER!
DEM JUDEN!

vor
JUDEN
u TASCHENDIEBEN
WIRD GEWARNT!

European nations protested that this action was illegal according to the Treaty of Versailles after World War I. But Great Britain, one of the protesters, did make a naval treaty with Hitler later that year, and this was but the first of many such agreements which overlooked Germany's defiance of law.

---

<table>
<tr><td>THE FOUR-YEAR<br>PLAN</td><td>In 1936, Hitler drafted a memorandum on military and economic preparations for war. It became known as the Four-Year Plan. Hitler felt Germany was ready for "the reconquest of freedom for</td></tr>
</table>

In 1936, Hitler drafted a memorandum on military and economic preparations for war. It became known as the Four-Year Plan. Hitler felt Germany was ready for "the reconquest of freedom for tomorrow." In his scheme, war was inevitable. "War is life," said Hitler in 1932. "War is the origin of all things." For Nazi Germany, war meant not simply conquering foreign territory or people, or economic wealth, but the means to acquire *Lebensraum*, that is, "living space." By Lebensraum, Hitler really meant space for racial supremacy. In *Mein Kampf* he wrote:

> *The foreign policy of the Volkist state must safeguard the existence on this planet of the race embodied in the state, by creating a healthy, viable natural relation between the nation's population and growth on the one hand and the quantity and quality of its soil on the other.*

That is, the superior German race must expand, so the land they will need must naturally grow as well.

Hitler believed that Germany was entitled to more land. Germany was the "mother of life," not just "some little nigger nation or other." War, despite its sacrifices, was therefore perfectly justifiable:

> *. . . we National Socialists must hold unflinchingly to our aim in foreign policy, namely, to secure for the German people the land and soil to which they are entitled on this earth. And this action is the only one which, before God and our German posterity, would make any sacrifice of blood seem justified. . . . The soil on which someday German generations of peasants can beget powerful sons will sanction the investment of the sons of today, and will someday acquit the responsible statesmen of blood-guilt and sacrifice of the people, even if they are persecuted by their contemporaries.*

Where would the soil come from? Some "lost territories" of pre-World War I days would be retaken. But only "new soil" would truly give Germany "a path to life." By "new soil" Hitler meant Russia. War meant conquering these enemies, but it also included a final earthshaking battle of the Aryan against the Jew. In fact, when Hitler spoke of war plans he frequently shifted the discussion into talk of murdering masses of Jews. It often appeared to his officers that war would be simply a cover-up for the destruction of Jewry.

The Four-Year Plan even provided for seizing Jewish property and wealth when Germany went to war. The Reichstag was to pass a law "making the whole of Jewry liable for all damage inflicted by individual specimens of this community of criminals upon the German economy, and thus upon the German people." With this authority, Göring would soon levy a tax on the Jews for the sum of one billion German marks.

Hitler was both cunning and patient in planning his war against the Jews. He discouraged his followers from rushing him to solve the Jewish question, but he assured them that he would carry out his plans. Hitler proclaimed that his enemies would suffer a "blow right in the heart," but not until he was ready. Thus Nazi foreign policy continued, and Hitler formed alliances with Italy, Japan, and the rebel government of General Franco in Spain. By 1937, Hitler was predicting he would conquer Austria and Czechoslovakia. In March 1938, the Nazis annexed Austria without even a single battle, and one year later the Germany Army marched into Czechoslovakia, again without encountering resistance. For Jews, every success of the Nazi war machine brought closer their impending doom.

The economic situation of the Jews had been continually worsening. Tens of thousands were out of work, Jewish businesses were being seized and "Aryanized" at an incredible pace, and Göring said that the final goal was that Jews "must be removed from the economy." In July 1938, Jews were required to carry identification cards at all times, and three months later passports for foreign travel were re-marked to indicate the holder as Jewish. Some Jewish organizations, like B'nai B'rith, were dissolved, while others were brought under police control. Jews were even restricted as to the names they might use—all males were to be called Israel, and all females Sarah.

Violent attacks on Jews and Jewish stores intensified. In Berlin, ". . . a gang of ten youngsters in Hitler Youth uniforms smashed the shop window and stormed into the shop, brandishing butcher knives and yelling: 'To hell with the Jewish rabble!'" Still worse, mass arrests led to the imprisoning of hundreds of Jews in Dachau, Buchenwald, and Sachsenhausen; these detention camps were beginning to

The ruins of the
synagogue on
Prinzregenten
Street in
Berlin-
Wilmersdorf,
Germany.

change into slave-labor camps. Many of the new prisoners were arrested for only one or two parking violations, but inmates at Dachau
were ordered to sew Stars of David on uniforms in preparation for
thousands more Jewish prisoners.

THE NIGHT OF
SHATTERED
GLASS

In the fall of 1938, violence against Jews in Germany hit an all-time
high. The Gestapo had been rounding up some fifty thousand Polish
Jews who were living in Germany, since neither the Germans nor
the Polish government would recognize them as citizens. The son of
one of the first couples to be arrested, Hershl Grynszpan, showed his
anger at these actions by assassinating a German official in Paris on
November 7, 1938. Two days later, the official died, and Nazis
throughout Germany had an excuse for hunting down Jewish "enemies
of the state." With Hitler's approval, and with Goebbels' active en-

The destroyed synagogue on Fasanen Street in Berlin-Charlottenburg, Germany.

couragement, fires were ignited throughout the country, and the streets were littered with broken glass from the windows of synagogues, Jewish stores, and homes. On that night of shattered glass, over seven thousand businesses were destroyed, nearly one hundred Jews were murdered, and thousands more were cruelly mistreated. About thirty thousand Jewish men were arrested and confined in Buchenwald, Dachau, and Sachsenhausen.

Now the government had its best opportunity, short of actual war, to deprive the Jews of their property and their freedom. Jewish businesses were not allowed to reopen unless they were to be managed by non-Jews. Jews were barred from most public places, like theatres and beaches, and Jewish children were expelled from German schools. The Jews, who were the main victims of the pogroms and looting, were blamed for them and required to pay one billion German marks in damages. According to the Nazi leadership, the main goal was still "to kick the Jew out of Germany."

Eichmann now tried to use terror to force Jewish emigration.

Within six months, forty-five thousand Jews were "encouraged" to leave Austria. Over one hundred thousand more would leave before war broke out. Eventually, Eichmann took over the Emigration and Evacuation desk of the political police, an office later renamed Jewish Affairs and Evacuation Affairs. In this position he would schedule, organize, and manage the deportation of European Jews to the death camps. Thus the Nazis changed over from expelling to exterminating Jews.

On January 21, 1939, Hitler told the Czech Foreign Minister: "We are going to destroy the Jews. . . . The day of reckoning has come." This message was confidential, but on January 30, 1939, Hitler used the anniversary of his coming to power to tell the Reichstag the same thing. This was his declaration of war against the Jews:

*And one more thing I would like now to state on this day*

*memorable perhaps not only for us Germans. I have often been
a prophet in my life and was generally laughed at. During my
struggle for power, the Jews primarily received with laughter
my prophecies that I would someday assume the leadership of
the state and thereby of the entire Volk and then, among
many other things, achieve a solution of the Jewish problem. I
suppose that meanwhile the then resounding laughter of
Jewry in Germany is now choking in their throats.*

      *Today I will be a prophet again: If international
finance Jewry within Europe and abroad should succeed once
more in plunging the peoples into a world war, then the
consequence will be not the Bolshevization of the world and
therewith a victory of Jewry, but on the contrary, the destruction of the Jewish race in Europe.*

---

**War is Life**   Hitler's belief that "war is life" is far different from the
Jewish concept of peace as fulfillment (the Hebrew word *shalom*,
שָׁלוֹם , comes from the root *shalem*, שלם , meaning "whole"). To
be sure, Jews have understood that war is sometimes necessary, but the
Bible legislates morality even during wartime: newly married men and
those who are too frightened to fight are exempted from battle; nonviolent means are always regarded as preferable to violence; and destroying fruit trees and other land resources is forbidden (Deuteronomy 20).
Maimonides, the foremost Jewish philosopher of the Middle Ages,
recorded the instances in which wars have to be fought, but he showed
that most war is unnecessary and wasteful in God's eyes. Of course,
this distinction was only theoretical since the Jews had not had armies
for centuries.

**The Treatment of Enemies**   It is natural to hate one's enemies. But
Jews have always taught that forgiveness and reconciliation are important; and even one's enemies must be treated with respect. Thus the
Bible demands that one return an enemy's lost animal and give aid
when an enemy's pack animal is lying helpless under its load (Exodus
23:4-5). I Kings 3:11 says God was pleased with Solomon because he
spared the lives of his enemies, and Proverbs 24:17 warns: "Do not
rejoice when your enemy falls." According to a Jewish legend, God was
displeased with the angels because they sang as the armies of Pharaoh
drowned in the Red Sea: "The work of My hands sinks into the sea, and
you would sing before Me? (Sanhedrin 39b)"

63

# CHAPTER EIGHT

# FROM INTERNAL WAR TO WORLD WAR

(Facing page) German troops ride through a battered Polish town after the Blitzkrieg in 1939.

Hitler's early invasions, first into Austria and then into Czechoslovakia, had been greeted with flowers, not guns. The British Prime Minister, Neville Chamberlain, at first told the House of Commons that Britain did not have to honor treaties and come to the defense of her European neighbors, but later he publicly admitted that Hitler had deceived and disappointed him. In March 1939, both the British and French governments announced that they would support Poland if Hitler tried to extend his power over Poland's borders.

This threat did not stop Hitler from planning to invade Poland, because he felt that he could not count on Poland's neutrality if he went to war with the Western powers. He wanted Germany to eliminate Poland through a lightning campaign *(Blitzkrieg)*, and he assured his officers that such an action would not lead to another war.

At the same time, Hitler was trying to make an alliance with Soviet Russia. Although Hitler had hated the Russians for years, he now hoped to protect his eastern flank in case of war with the West. The Russians showed their interest by suddenly dismissing Foreign Minister Maxim Litvinov, who represented everything the Germans hated — he was a Jew, a peace advocate, a supporter of the League of Nations, a friend of the Western democracies, and an opponent of the Nazis. Hitler was now anxious to do business with his former enemies, as he put it, to make a "pact with Satan so as to drive out the Devil."

By the summer of 1939, everything was "go" for the invasion of Poland. Plans were made for expanding concentration camps to hold

prisoners who would become slave laborers for the German war machine. On August 23 the Soviets signed a trade agreement with the Nazis and agreed secretly that Poland should be divided between their two countries. Two days later, Britain signed a formal treaty with Poland, but Hitler delayed his invasion for only a week. At 6:30 A.M. on September 1, 1939, German troops invaded Poland all along the frontier.

On September 3, Britain declared war on Germany, and a few hours later France followed. That same day Prime Minister Chamberlain broadcast the news. "It is evil things we shall be fighting against: brute force, bad faith, injustice, oppression, and persecution. But against them I am certain that the right will prevail."

Poland was no match for the Germans, and by September 17 the western half of Poland was in German hands except for Warsaw, which was holding out heroically against a siege. Ten days later Warsaw gave in, and by then Russia had overrun the eastern Polish territories. The conquerors signed a German-Soviet Boundary and Friendship Treaty and issued a public declaration saying that they had created "a firm foundation for a lasting peace in Eastern Europe." They also called for England and France to end the state of war against Germany.

---

THE
OCCUPATION
OF POLAND

The occupation of Poland at last gave Hitler the opportunity to begin the racial programs he had planned for two decades. Hitler promoted Himmler, who now became virtual master of Poland, and his SS took charge of the war against the Jews. As Hitler put it, the "old and new Reich area" was to be "cleansed of Jews, Polacks, and company." Racial screening would bring "racially valuable" Aryan types from Poland to Germany for Nazi indoctrination, while nearly one-half million "racially pure" Germans were settled in colonies from which Poles were expelled. Hitler saw these measures as a "tough struggle for national existence" that "permits no legal restraints." The Polish leadership was to be killed, and the Jews were to be segregated in a few large centers as a first step toward their destruction.

The SS were particularly responsible for inhuman treatment of the Jews, but even ordinary army officers were being taught to believe in a double standard of combat, where the Jew was the most hated enemy. An army briefing booklet entitled "The Jew in German History" shows how the army accepted Nazi ideas:

October 1, 1939. A column of troops enters the Theatre Square in Warsaw, Poland.

*We Germans fight a twofold fight today. With regard to the non-Jewish peoples we want only to accomplish our vital interests. We respect them and conduct a chivalrous argument with them. But we fight world Jewry as one has to fight a poisonous parasite; we encounter in him not only the enemy of our people, but a plague of all peoples. The fight against Jewry is a moral fight for the purity and health of God-created humanity and for a new more just order in the world.*

Heydrich now drafted orders for racial policies in Poland. Jews were to be concentrated in city ghettos "for a better possibility of control and later possibility of deportation." Jews and Gypsies were to be moved as quickly as possible out of the German Reich and into Poland. And in each community a Jewish council *(Judenrat)* was to be established to be "fully responsible" for prompt and careful coopera-tion with all government decrees. The final aim of these policies, however, was not to create in Poland (or even in Africa, as some had suggested) a "reservation" for the Jews. Rather, the Nazi racial pro-gram called for only one Final Solution of the Jewish Question—total extermination. Poland was Hitler's testing ground for these plans, but first he had to cope with Russia.

**H**itler had always thought about waging war against Russia. But first he had to turn his attention to the West. In April 1940, the Nazis invaded Denmark and Norway; in May, the Netherlands, Belgium, and France. When the French surrendered on June 21, 1940, Hitler stood triumphant at the English Channel, planning to invade Great Britain by September.

Meanwhile, Hitler watched as the Soviets massed large forces in the East, and early in July he ordered his staff to make Polish roads, railroad lines, and airfields ready for the German army to push eastward. The sea invasion of Britain had to be delayed, because the British air force was still superior to Hitler's. Barely fifteen months after signing the German-Soviet Boundary and Friendship Treaty, Hitler ordered: "The German armed forces must be prepared, even before the conclusion of the war against England, to crush Soviet Russia in a rapid campaign."

The battle against Russia had special importance to Hitler, because it pitted the Aryans against an "opposing political system" of Jewish Bolshevism. Thus, a top secret decree gave the SS *Einsatzgruppen,* Special Duty Groups, authority to kill all the Jews in the territory conquered by the German Army. At about this same time, Himmler visited Auschwitz to give its commandant, Rudolf Höss, instructions to expand its facilities to hold one hundred thousand prisoners of war in addition to thirty thousand "peacetime" prisoners. By prisoners of war, Himmler did not mean captured soldiers of the enemy army but "politically intolerable elements," like Soviet state officials, Communist party leaders, and especially Jews.

After capturing Yugoslavia in April 1941 and Greece one month later, Hitler was ready to take on the Russians. His plans were merciless. "It is a question of war of destruction. . . . We do not conduct war to conserve the enemy." The battle against Russia was to be so desperate that German soldiers were instructed to ignore the niceties of international law when dealing with prisoners. "This struggle demands ruthless and energetic measures against Bolshevik agitators, guerillas, saboteurs, Jews, and the complete elimination of every active or passive resistance." After the German army had invaded Russia, the generals instructed their soldiers that the "most essential aim of the campaign against the Jewish-Bolshevist system is the complete crushing of its means of power. . . . Therefore the soldier must have full understanding for the necessity of a severe but just atonement on Jewish subhumanity."

While these were the orders to regular troops, the new

Nazi soldiers lead Jewish women into the woods for execution. This was the pattern of the *Einsatzgruppen* who carried out similar executions throughout Eastern Europe.

Special Duty Groups received even more intensive indoctrination. Organized in divisions of eight-hundred to twelve-hundred men, their special task was to kill the Jews. These instructions were always given orally, never in writing, but it was clear that they came directly from the Führer. When the German armed forces drove into Russia on June 22, 1941, with or right behind them came four waves of Special Duty Groups, divided north to south.

Russian resistance crumbled quickly, and the Special Duty Groups went to work with skill, terror, and systematic savagery.

*[They] would enter a village or city and order the prominent Jewish citizens to call together all Jews for the purpose of resettlement. They were requested to hand over their valuables to the leader of the unit, and shortly before the execution to surrender their outer clothing. The men, women, and children were led to a place of execution which in most cases was located next to a more deeply excavated anti-tank ditch. Then*

69

A French cartoon shows Hitler as an octopus trying to encircle the whole world.

*they were shot kneeling or standing, and the corpses thrown into the ditch.*

At Nuremberg after the war, the International Military Tribunal concluded that of approximately six million Jews murdered, two million were killed by the Special Duty Groups and other units of the SS..

---

ISSUES AND
VALUES

**The Role of International Law**    Wars between nations often result from a series of illegal acts by one or more of the governments involved. Hitler broke international law because he believed (contrary to the law) that Germany was entitled to more land and more power, and eventually to world dominion. The Nazis valued their ideas of racial superiority above any legal system, and for many years the western world lacked the inclination or the power to stop Germany's crimes.

Ironically, the Jews who were the principal victims of Hitler's crimes have a centuries-old commitment to justice and law. In Jewish tradition, God gave the law, and the rabbis are its interpreters and commentators. According to the Mishnah, the law is an important source of moral behavior which teaches the world to strive for peace and salvation (Gittin 4:3-5; 5:8-9). In this sense, Jewish law was not viewed as being for the Jews alone to observe. God first made His convenant with all the peoples of the earth through Adam and through Noah, the ancestors of all nations, and all nations are expected to observe at least seven laws: the prohibitions against idolatry, murder, theft, blasphemy, incest, and eating the flesh of a living animal, and the obligation to promote justice.

**A Pact with Satan**　Jewish tradition claims that God makes demands of all people, demands which are essential to human welfare. When the Bible speaks of sin, it uses words with meanings such as "to fall," "to miss the mark," or "to twist or rebel." Thus people sin when they commit deeds prohibited by God's law or when they fall short of doing what the law demands. Sometimes Hitler defended his actions by saying that he had "made a pact with Satan to drive out the Devil"; that is "the end justifies the means." But the ancient rabbis argued that one must not sin even in order to perform God's commandments. For example, one must not steal candles in order to have candles to light on the Sabbath, for how can one use stolen goods to worship God?

# CHAPTER NINE

# THE ANNIHILATION CAMPS: KINGDOM OF DEATH

**(Facing page) Inmates of Buchenwald freed by the Allied troops peer from their wooden bunks.**

Sometime in the spring or summer of 1941, Hitler gave Himmler and the SS responsibility for the Final Solution of the Jewish Question. In the late summer of 1941, Himmler told his men that those "who were taking part in the liquidation bore no personal responsibility for the execution of this order. The responsibility was his alone, and the Führer's." A year later, Himmler wrote to a top SS official that "the occupied Eastern territories are to become free of Jews."

While the Final Solution was ultimately Himmler's responsibility, his colleague, Heydrich, was in charge of administrative details, and Eichmann became the supervisor of "Jewish Affairs and Evacuation Affairs." Auschwitz was chosen to be expanded as the major death camp because it was both isolated and easy to reach by rail. Eichmann discussed with Auschwitz administrator, Höss, plans for scheduling the murder of the Jews and the techniques of killing to be used—some form of gassing. Mass killing by gas had already been developed, under Hitler's supervision, in order to get rid of "racially unhealthy" parts of the population. By the spring of 1939, Hitler had already regularized a program for killing mentally deficient and physically deformed children. About five thousand children were murdered during this program, which lasted until November 1944.

Once set in motion the official destruction of what Nazi ideology called the "racially valueless" children, Hitler next turned to the "medical" murder of the adult insane, which would become an

Ovens at
Buchenwald.

even bigger program. Patients were first sent to one of five "observation institutions," then to one of six "mercy-killing" centers. While the deformed children were put to death individually, usually by injection, these six centers became the German dictatorship's first laboratories for mass murder.

A committee of medical experts was assigned to find a means of mass killing that would deceive both the victims and their

74

families. Various gasses were tried and the procedure was relatively simple and convincingly deceptive. In groups of twenty to thirty, the patients were brought into a chamber disguised as a shower room. The doors and windows of the room were sealed, and the patients, who believed they were there for showers, were instead gassed to death by the doctor on duty. It did not take long before people learned what was going on, as the heavy smoke rose every day from the crematory building. After more than a year of public outcry in Germany, Hitler decided in August 1941 to "stall" the killing of mental patients. But these experiments in mass murder had already taken between eighty thousand and one hundred thousand victims.

---

In the summer of 1941 construction began on a series of death camps, including Birkenau, which would become Auschwitz's killing center. The first facility to be completed was Chełmno, which was intended for the Jews of the ghetto in nearby Lodz. Gassing began there in December 1941, with mobile vans. By mid-1942, there were new gassing installations at Belżec, Majdanek, and Treblinka. At the same time, experts argued over whether gassing or shooting was "more honorable" in mass killing.

On January 20, 1942, Heydrich assembled a group of thirteen state and party officials for a conference in a small, private villa located in Am Grossen Wannsee, a suburb of Berlin. The Wannsee Conference gave Heydrich, assisted by Eichmann who served as secretary, a chance to brief various important agencies on the plans for the Final Solution. He reviewed the shift in Nazi policy from "emigration" to "evacuation" (a bloodless way of saying "murder"), and then raised the problem of how to proceed with the destruction of Jews in the many foreign European countries. Europe had "to be combed through from west to east" for Jews, who would be sent first to "transit ghettos" and then to death camps.

There would be a few exceptions—German Jews over sixty-five and World War I veterans who had been wounded or had performed distinguished service would be assigned to a ghetto for the aged. The site Heydrich chose was Theresienstadt, which eventually became a "model camp," a false front the Germans used to deceive foreign visitors. Among its inmates were many prominent German Jews whose disappearance would prove embarrassing in the case of international inquiries about their welfare. But in reality, Theresienstadt for most of its inmates was just a stopping place before their final destination at Auschwitz.

Other discussions at the Wannsee Conference centered on what to do with *Mischlinge,* people who because they had a Jewish ancestor were partially Jewish, and Jews working in industries vital to the war effort. It was decided that some categories of Mischlinge would be killed if they had an "especially unfavorable appearance in racial terms," and Jews in essential war-time jobs would not be "evacuated." In practice, however, anyone with any Jewish ancestry, regardless of job, had much to fear from the SS.

With the technical and administrative plans completed, the Final Solution began. Often with terror and force, SS Special Duty Groups began to bring Jews from all over Europe to the death camps. Sometimes, victims were deceived into believing they were going for "resettlement for work in the East." Offers of bread and marmalade brought thousands of volunteers for "resettlement" from the starving ghettos of Poland. But "resettlement" really meant transport to the gas chambers. On March 27, 1942, Goebbels wrote in his diary: "The procedure is a pretty barbaric one. . . . Not much will remain of the Jews."

From as far as Greece and Russia, in cities like Vienna and Prague, and in numbers ranging into the hundreds of thousands, whole communities of Jews were seized and sent to their deaths. From 1942 to 1944, the SS often competed with the regular army for the railroad cars, and usually the Final Solution took priority even over the war effort. The army administrators opposed the "larger executions" because Jewish skilled labor was very much needed, but the commanders of the Special Duty Groups responded "that it was a matter of carrying out basic orders."

As long as the Jews were permitted to live, they were forced to labor without reward or mercy. After their deportation, the Germans took their remaining possessions. Money and precious jewels stolen from the Jews were deposited in the Reichsbank. Watches, wallets, pens and pencils, razors, and scissors were sold to the army troops. Clothing, bedding, and even personal items like eyeglasses, combs, mirrors, and canes were priced and sold. A balance sheet of goods accumulated between April 1, 1942 and December 15, 1943 showed the income from these items to be about 180 million Reichsmarks.

Arriving at Auschwitz, Bełżec, Chełmno, Majdanek,

(Facing page) Wedding rings confiscated by the Nazis from Jews murdered in the death camps.

Sobibór, and Treblinka, the Jews faced a standard procedure. At camps with labor installations, the ten percent who looked fittest were selected for work, and the rest were gassed. They were told to undress, and the women and girls had their hair cut. Then they marched between files of police who hurried them along with whips, sticks, or guns to the gas chambers. Into these "shower rooms" they were rammed, one person per square foot. Ten to thirty minutes later, depending on the facility and gas used, all were dead. To make room for the next load, the bodies were tossed out right away, to be burned later either in crematoria or the open air. "At night the red sky over Auschwitz could be seen for miles."

The statistics of the death camps can only be approximate. Most victims were Jews, but also all Gypsies and thousands of non-Jews — selected for particular reasons — were gassed.

| | |
|---|---|
| Auschwitz | 2,000,000 |
| Bełżec | 600,000 |
| Chełmno | 340,000 |
| Majdanek | 1,380,000 |
| Sobibór | 250,000 |
| Treblinka | 800,000 |
| TOTAL | 5,370,000 |

On October 4, 1943, Himmler spoke about the SS and the Final Solution to a group of military officers:

*I also want to refer before you here, in complete frankness, to a really grave matter. Among ourselves, this once, it shall be uttered quite frankly; but in public we will never speak of it. . . .*

*I am referring to the evacuation of the Jews, the annihilation of the Jewish people. This is one of those things that are easily said. "The Jewish people is going to be annihilated," says every party member. "Sure, it's in our program, elimination of the Jews, annihilation — we'll take care of it." And then they all come trudging, eighty million worthy Germans, and each one has his one decent Jew. Sure, the others are swine, but this one is an A-1 Jew. Of all those who talk this way, not one has seen it happen, not one has been through it. Most of you must know what it means to see a hundred corpses lie side by side, or five hundred, or a thou-*

*sand. To have stuck this out and—excepting cases of human
weakness—to have kept our integrity, this is what has made
us hard. In our history, this is an unwritten and never-to-be-
written page of glory. . . .*

---

**Pikuaḥ Nefesh (Saving Life)**   When two values conflict, we must
choose which is more urgent or precious. From biblical times onward,
Jewish sources have regarded the saving of human life as the most
precious value of all. Leviticus 18:5 declares, "You must keep [God's]
institutions and laws; the person who keeps them shall have life
through them." The rabbis took this verse to mean that even the
Sabbath, one of God's most important institutions and the only one
mentioned in the Ten Commandments, may be set aside in order to
preserve life (Shabbat 2:5, Yoma 75a), and that health is more important than ritual (Hullin 10a). Many other ancient peoples practice
human sacrifice to appease their gods, but Jews regarded this sort of
"worship" as repugnant.

   In the Nazi world, one can see the small value which was
placed on the life of an individual human being. Even German lives
were considered less important than the success of Hitler's scheme to
rule the world. By contrast, the Jewish tradition maintains that the
saving of one life is like the saving of the entire universe.

**Thou Shalt Not Murder**   The Bible records the legend of Cain and
Abel to show that murder is to be regarded as a terrible crime. Later,
the prohibition is explained to Noah: "He that sheds the blood of a
person, for that person his blood shall be shed; for in the image of God
has God made man (Genesis 9:6)." This prohibition against murder is
repeated in the Ten Commandments, where it is the first of the five
commandments which apply to the ways in which people must treat one
another. Of course, the Bible distinguishes between accidental murder
(manslaughter) and intentional murder (Numbers 35:16-24), but the
Jewish tradition clearly abhors any taking of human life.

   Even capital punishment, the taking of the murderer's life in
exchange for the life he has taken, was to be avoided wherever
possible. The rabbis created so many exemptions and special rules
that had to be followed in cases of murder that some rabbis believed it
almost impossible for a rabbinic court to put anyone to death.

# CHAPTER TEN

# LOOKING BACK

The Final Solution began in Hitler's mind. In *Mein Kampf* he says that he decided to go to war against the Jews in November 1918. Then a patient in a military hospital, he heard of Germany's defeat in World War I. "Everything went black before my eyes," he wrote. "Terrible days and even worse nights" followed as he struggled to understand what had happened. Then "my own fate became known to me." He decided: "There is no making pacts with Jews; there can only be the hard: either—or. I, for my part, decided to go into politics."

We will never know whether Hitler really decided then, in November 1918, on the destruction of the Jews as his political goal, or whether the idea remained buried in his mind until it took shape in *Mein Kampf*, written in 1924. *Mein Kampf* was Hitler's major statement, in which he brought together three ideas that added up to the Final Solution. First, he turned political anti-Semitism into a racial doctrine which demanded destruction of the Jews. Second, he defined Bolshevism as a Jewish conspiracy for world rule and preached a crusade to "liberate" Russia from its supposedly Jewish masters. Third, he used the idea of Aryan racial superiority to argue that German imperialism was a righteous effort to win "living space" for Germans. Thus, Hitler took common political notions and wove them together into an incredibly radical program for the annihilation of world Jewry.

If Hitler formed his plans much before he wrote *Mein*

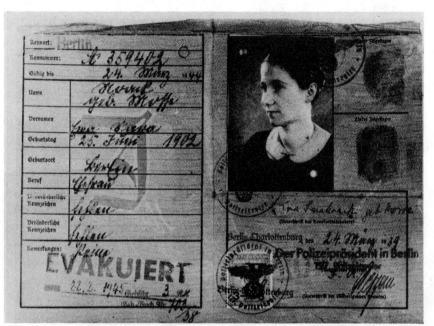

All Jews were required to carry an identity card marked with a large J for *Jude*—Jew.

*Kampf*, he could have talked about them only secretly or in some vague way. His message was revolutionary, even for ordinary anti-Semites. Hitler complained in *Mein Kampf* that he had difficulties in the early days. "Our first attempts," he wrote, "to show the public the real enemy then seemed almost hopeless." The problem was that his National Socialists did not want to be dismissed as "crackpot" anti-Semites who had no political solutions for contemporary problems. In public, Hitler had to use his public speaking talents carefully, avoiding "plain references" to the Jews.

In Nazi meetings, however, the word "Jew" could be used without limit or caution. Still, Hitler often preferred code words like "exploiters," "capitalists," "international money power," "Communists," "revolution criminals," and "foreigners." When he talked about the press, it was clear he meant the Jewish press. In general, he was able to tell the "insiders" how to understand the "Jewish conspiracy," and his speeches made clear that all of Germany's enemies were Jews or tools of Jews.

How would he deal with this enemy? In his early speeches Hitler preferred to use terms like "removal," "elimination," and "cleaning up." On April 27, 1920, Hitler closed a speech by saying,

"We will carry on the struggle until the last Jew is removed from the German Reich." Since he used such vague language, it is possible that his listeners believed he meant only to expel the Jews from Germany, not to murder them.

In an early letter, Hitler wrote: "Rational anti-Semitism . . . must lead to a systematic legal opposition and elimination of the special privileges that Jews hold, in contrast to the other aliens living among us. Its final objective must unswervingly be the removal of the Jews altogether." Here Hitler says that Germany must first deprive Jews of all rights—and then, finally, "remove" them entirely. He deliberately allows the reader to interpret exactly what the "removal" means. Similarly, in a speech on April 12, 1922, he referred to the Jewish question by saying: "There are only two possibilities: either victory of the Aryan or annihilation of the Aryan and the victory of the Jew." Clearly, Hitler meant for his listener to understand that victory for the Aryan made necessary something he did not mention; namely, annihilation of the Jew. In 1922 Hitler used vague language to speak about killing Jews, and in 1939 he would use the same kind of "saying without really saying" to talk about conquering the world.

---

THE
INTERNATIONAL
STRUGGLE

In his early years, Hitler seems to have confined his plans only to German Jews, who had to be "removed" in order to "purify" Germany's racial strength. But soon he began to see the Jews more as an international group whose destruction demanded an international policy. In 1922, he explained in a party speech that "two worlds are struggling with one another, and not alone in our country, but everywhere we look. . . . How long will it be before the whole world falls to ruin?"

Hitler was able to expand his program to an international one by identifying the Jews with Russia. Germany could properly invade Russia in order to free it from the "Jew-Bolshevik" Communists. The "eastern marches of Germany," as Hitler put it, through Poland and into Russia, were also justified on racial grounds. The Aryan needed more "living space," and the racially inferior Jews would therefore have to be overcome and displaced. Hitler probably took the idea of "living space" from the losses Germany suffered in World War I. But while many Germans agreed that territory, natural resources, and other material assets were needed, it was Hitler who provided the racial theory to defend a new war effort to acquire those things.

Writing *Mein Kampf* in 1924 and 1925 forced Hitler to put down his random ideas in a more organized fashion. The single unifying theme for foreign and domestic policy is the war against the Jews. Time and again, he advocates destroying the Jews, now in language which is quite clear:

> *Only the elimination of the causes of our collapse, as well as the destruction of its beneficiaries, can create the premise for our outward fight for freedom.*
>
> *. . . It is the inexorable Jew who struggles for his domination over the nations. No nation can remove this hand from its throat except by the sword. Only the assembled and concentrated might of a national passion rearing up in its strength can defy the international enslavement of peoples. Such a process is and remains a bloody one.*

At the same time, Hitler made the Jew over in his own image: "The Jew would really devour the people of the earth, would become their master." He even argued that a "preventive" war against the Jews in 1914–1918 would have saved Germany from defeat in World War I.

> *If the best men were dying at the front, the least we could do was to wipe out the vermin.*
>
> *If at the beginning of the War and during the War twelve or fifteen thousand of these Hebrew corrupters of the people had been held under poison gas . . . the sacrifice of millions at the front would not have been in vain. On the contrary: twelve thousand scoundrels eliminated in time might have saved the lives of a million real Germans, valuable for the future.*

In the years between 1919 and 1925, the political climate in Germany had changed, and Hitler could now make his plans straightforward and public. But only his followers took his words literally, while others who listened to him or read *Mein Kampf* believed Hitler to be a raving fool. Yet these words became policies when he came to power, and soon thereafter they astonishingly became political and military reality.

**T**he Final Solution grew out of the combination of traditional anti-Semitism, the paranoid delusions that seized Germany after World War I, and the rise of Hitler and the Nazis. Without this social atmosphere, this political situation, and this charismatic, driven leader, officially sponsored mass murder would never have been possible. Anti-Semitism was the core of Hitler's beliefs and the central motive for his policies. He believed himself to be the savior of Germany who would rescue it from what he believed were the Satanic forces of world Jewry. The murder of the Jews was his "holy mission," and he spoke often as a prophet of "salvation" and "God's will." Until his death in a Berlin bunker, he held to the fantasy expressed most clearly in *Mein Kampf:* "By defending myself against the Jews, I am fighting for the work of the Lord."

Generations of anti-Semitism had prepared the Germans to accept Hitler as their redeemer. Layer upon layer of Christian church teachings about the Jews, Volkist anti-Semitism, doctrines of racial superiority, economic theories about the roles of Jews in capitalism and commerce, and a half-century of political anti-Semitism climaxed in the Nazi movement. The insecurity of Germany after World War I provided the emotional setting in which hysteria became routine. Masses of Germans were unable to distinguish between real and mythic Jews. What Germans hated and feared most in themselves, the drive for power, they projected onto the Jews. The Jew became a germ to be wiped out, and a mortal enemy to be killed in self-defense. The Aryan "superhuman" was in a death struggle against what Hitler believed to be a Jewish conspiracy to rule the world.

Hitler skillfully translated this imaginary war into a real one. On April 15, 1945, when six million Jews had already been murdered, he issued his last military order. He called for his troops to perform their utmost. "For the last time our mortal enemies the Jewish Bolsheviks have launched their massive forces to the attack. Their aim is to reduce Germany to ruins and to exterminate our people." But only the truly mad could have believed that it was war that they were waging against the Jews. For the Jews were civilians, dispersed among the European nations, having no country and no political power, and therefore none of the resources that even small nations could muster for war.

**The Power of Truth**    Hitler's government was, to a large extent, built on falsehood and deception. The Nazis feared truth, because they knew that few other nations would willingly accept the idea that Germany represented the "Master Race." German officials were careful not to speak or write publicly about the Final Solution, for they knew that world opinion would never tolerate such a scheme.

The ancient rabbis believed that the world itself could not be sustained without truth (Avot 1:18). The Book of Proverbs repeats the idea that truth endures, whereas falsehood brings grief (12:19; 17:20).

Ultimately, though far too late, the truth about Germany and the Nazi program was made known and the civilized world rose against the Germans. The rabbis of the Talmud were so convinced that truth would ultimately prevail that they called truth "the seal of God (Shabbat 55a)."

**Kiddush Hashem (Sanctification of God's Name)**    Jews often have been forced to choose between forsaking their faith and sacrificing their lives in the hope that Judaism as a way of life would not perish. From the time of the Maccabean Revolt some twenty-one hundreds years ago (II Maccabees 6–7) to our own days, many have chosen to take their own lives rather than convert to another religion or be forced to live in slavery. In some cases, particularly during the Holocaust, Jews were given no choice whatever.

Sanctifying the name of God, that is, witnessing to God's holiness and presence, is usually accomplished through prayer. Many prayers are set aside for this purpose and their names come from the Hebrew word for "holiness," *kadosh*, קָדוֹשׁ  —such as the *kiddush*, קִדּוּשׁ , the *kedushah*, קְדוּשָׁה , and the *kaddish* קַדִּישׁ . God's name may also be sanctified through charity and acts of loving kindness. Acts of holiness are commanded by God, according to the Bible, because Israel must strive to be holy just as the Lord is holy (Leviticus 19:2; 23:21). Thus, when it comes to a point where living means giving up one's way of life, a way of life sanctified in holiness, death itself can become a way of sanctifying God's name on earth. The Jewish term for this martyrdom is *Kiddush Hashem*, קִדּוּשׁ הַשֵּׁם .

# DOCUMENTS OF THE FINAL SOLUTION

The Holocaust is one of the best-documented events in human history. When the historian wants to know what happened, when, and why, there is a sea of official records and private papers ready to be investigated. Naturally, sources must be studied carefully; some may lie, others may exaggerate, and all will need interpretation. The documents reproduced here and in "Documents of the Holocaust" (pp. 180–186) are meant to give a taste of the historian's tools and task, as well as to bring the chapters of this book into sharper focus.

In 1945, the Western Allies used the captured German state records to bear witness against the crimes of Hitler's Germany. After the trials began, the United States decided to make these captured German and Nazi records available also for research. The National Archives in Washington, D.C. prepared microfilms of some fifteen million pages of official Nazi documents. From these materials, the United States selected the most important to give as evidence before the International Military Tribunal at Nuremberg. In the same way, Great Britain, France, and the Soviet Union all prepared and submitted evidence. The record of the trial of major war criminals, along with all the documents submitted in evidence, was published—in identical English, French, and German versions—in forty-two volumes.

Twelve proceedings before the Nuremberg tribunal followed the trial of the major war criminals, and in all some three thousand documents were introduced as evidence of Nazi persecution and annihilation of the Jews. Not all of these documents were governmental accounts, since the treatment of the Jews was often not a matter of public record. Additional evidence came from the eyewitness testimony of individual Germans, who wished to protest their innocence, to claim that they had not participated in the Final Solution.

---

1. The Nazi quest to destroy the Jewish people began with Hitler's "conversion" to anti-Semitism. *Mein Kampf* records Hitler's early "investigation" of the Jews, when he concluded that Jews were a racial group and not a religious community. He called them physically dirty and morally corrupt; and claimed that their mere existence threatened to "pollute" Germany.

HITLER'S "CONVERSION" (FROM *MEIN KAMPF*)
... I could no longer very well doubt that the objects of my study were not Germans of a special religion, but a people in themselves; for since I had begun to concern myself with this question and to take cognizance of the Jews, Vienna appeared to me in a different light than

before. Wherever I went, I began to see Jews, and the more I saw, the more sharply they became distinguished in my eyes from the rest of humanity.

. . . By their very exterior you could tell that these were no lovers of water, and, to your distress, you often knew it with your eyes closed. . . . Added to this, there was their unclean dress and their generally unheroic appearance.

. . . This was pestilence, spiritual pestilence, worse than the Black Death of olden times, and the people was being infected with it!

. . . It was terrible, but not to be overlooked, that precisely the Jew, in tremendous numbers, seemed chosen by Nature for this shameful calling.

Is this why the Jews are called the "chosen people"?

---

2. To begin the Final Solution, Hitler had to win the aid of the German people. The technique he used to gain power and then transform his government into a dictatorship was propaganda. Hitler planned this aspect of his war against the Jews, as everything else he did, very carefully. And the "big lie" proved very successful indeed, not only in Germany but around the globe.

All propaganda must be popular and its intellectual level must be adjusted to the most limited intelligence among those it is addressed to. Consequently, the greater the mass it is intended to reach, the lower its purely intellectual level will have to be. But if, as in propaganda for sticking out a war, the aim is to influence a whole people, we must avoid excessive intellectual demands on our public, and too much caution cannot be exerted in this direction.

PROPAGANDA (FROM *MEIN KAMPF*)

---

3. Hitler violently hated the Jews from early in his life, and he developed cunning and efficient ways of spreading his anti-Semitism. Now the vicious lies which he proclaimed about the Jewish people and Judaism may be understood in their proper place. One such distorted claim was that the Jews are not a real, civilized people at all, but merely "parasites" living off others.

Hence the Jewish people, despite all apparent intellectual qualities is without any true culture, and especially without any culture of its own. For what sham culture the Jew today possesses is the property of other peoples, and for the most part it is ruined in his hands.

. . . There has never been a Jewish art and accordingly there

JEWISH CULTURE (FROM *MEIN KAMPF*)

is none today either. . . . We owe nothing original to the Jews. What they do accomplish in the field of art is either patchwork or intellectual theft. Thus, the Jew lacks those qualities which distinguish the races that are creative and hence culturally blessed.

---

4. After arguing against the existence of any distinct and original Jewish culture, Hitler goes on to attack the idea of the Jews as a religious community. He calls the Jews "unjust," "greedy," and "unworthy of emancipation."

JEWISH RELIGION AND LOYALTY (FROM *MEIN KAMPF*)

. . . The Jew of all times has lived in the states of other peoples, and there formed his own state, which, to be sure, habitually sailed under the disguise of "religious community" as long as outward circumstances made a complete revelation of his nature seem advisable.

. . . Indeed, things can go so far that large parts of the host people will end by seriously believing that the Jew is really a Frenchman or an Englishman, a German or an Italian, though of a special religious faith.

. . . Here, too, everything is borrowed or rather stolen. Due to his original special nature the Jew cannot possess a religious institution, if for no other reason because he lacks idealism in any form, and hence belief in a hereafter is absolutely foreign to him. . . . Indeed, the Talmud is not a book to prepare a man for the hereafter, but only for a practical and profitable life in this world.

---

5. Hitler's war against the Jews became a world war, and Heinrich Himmler became one of the chief architects of that effort. Himmler charged his SS leaders to pay any price necessary for a German victory, and he warned that no cost was too great if the result would be an Aryan triumph.

CHARGE TO SS LEADERS (FROM A SPEECH BY HIMMLER, OCTOBER 4, 1943)

One basic principle must be absolute for the SS man: we must be honest, decent, loyal, and comradely to members of our own blood and to nobody else. What happens to the Russians, what happens to the Czechs, is a matter of total indifference to me. What there is among the nations in the way of good blood of our kind, we will take for ourselves—if necessary, by kidnapping their children and raising them among us. Whether the other nations live in prosperity or croak from hunger interests me only insofar as we need them as slaves for our culture; otherwise, it does not interest me. Whether ten thousand Russian females drop from exhaustion while building an anti-tank ditch interests me only insofar as the anti-tank ditch gets finished for Germany's sake. We shall never be brutal and heartless where it is not necessary — obviously not. We Germans, the only people in the world who have a decent attitude toward animals, will also take a decent attitude toward these human animals. But it is a crime against our own blood to worry about them and to give them ideals that will make it still harder for our sons and grandsons to cope with them. If someone were to come to me and say, "I cannot build the anti-tank ditch with women or children; it is inhuman, they will die in the process," then I would have to say, "You are a murderer of your own blood, for if the anti-tank ditch is not built, German soldiers will die, and they are sons of German mothers. They are our own blood." This is what I want to instill into the SS and what I believe I have instilled into them as one of the most sacred laws of the future: Our concern, our duty is to our people and our blood; it is for them that we have to provide and to plan, to work and to fight, and for nothing else. Toward anything else we can be indifferent.

---

6. Germany's assault on European Jewry was masked by its military struggle against its neighbors, but other governments and world Jewish leaders were not unaware of Hitler's intent to annihilate the Jews. It is difficult to know how much more could have been done to save Hitler's victims, but the evidence clearly shows that many governments stood by while the death camps proceeded with their gruesome task. Early in the Nazi regime, United States consulates began to send official reports of anti-Jewish persecution back to the State Department in Washington.

*April 10*

"It is the undisguished intention of the National Socialist Party to get absolute control of all forms of German Government and of intellectual, professional, financial, business, and cultural life. . . . The forcing of the Jewish judges from the courts . . . are brought about by Party pressure and action. . . . It is a question as to whether such direct ruthless and complete control of a civilized people has ever been achieved in so short a time by a minority."

DISPATCHES FROM GERMANY (FROM U.S. CONSULATES, 1933)

*May 4*

"Not only careers, but whole families are being ruined and the moral and physical distress which has resulted out of this action against the Jews in the legal profession would be difficult to describe."

[Regarding book burning scheduled for May 10 at all universities]: "This ceremony which is to be given wide publicity seems to be as medieval in form as it seems in spirit. . . . The state of mind of the Jews from the highest to the lowest in Germany is difficult to describe and I can only state that I have come in contact in the past few months here with moral suffering such as I have not seen anywhere and under any conditions heretofore."

*July 8*
"Consistently and relentlessly the Jews are being eliminated from practically all walks of life." Nazi doctors and lawyers are "conducting bitter, relentless boycott against their Jewish colleagues. . . . Nazi leaders have repeatedly boasted in the past that one of the first acts of a Nazi regime would be to set up ghettos in Germany. . . . the outward and official manifestations of anti-Semitism in present-day Germany fail to reveal the real brutality and truculence of the Nazis toward the Jews, and that they are determined to make life for Jews in Germany well-nigh insufferable."

---

7. Despite the dire messages from Jewish and official sources in Europe, the United States was slow to come to the aid of European Jewry. How was Hitler able to implement his most horrible plans without incurring military intervention by the Americans? One reason appears to be that certain State Department officials deliberately suppressed information concerning events in Europe. These misdeeds were exposed by three officials in the United States Department of the Treasury, who in early 1944 submitted an eighteen-page document to Secretary of the Treasury Morganthau for presentation to President Roosevelt.

EXCERPTS FROM THE REPORT TO THE SECRETARY (OF THE TREASURY) ON THE ACQUIESCENCE OF THIS GOVERNMENT TO THE MURDER OF THE JEWS

[State Department officials] have not only failed to use the Governmental machinery at their disposal to rescue Jews from Hitler, but have even gone so far as to use this Governmental machinery to prevent the rescue of these Jews.

They have not only failed to cooperate with private organizations in the efforts of these organizations to work out individual programs of their own, but have taken steps designed to prevent these programs from being put into effect.

They not only have failed to facilitate the obtaining of information concerning Hitler's plans to exterminate the Jews of Europe but in their official capacity have gone so far as to surreptitiously attempt to stop the obtaining of information concerning the murder of the Jewish population of Europe.

They have tried to cover up their guilt by:

(a) concealment and misrepresentation;

(b) the giving of false and misleading explanations for their failures to act and their attempts to prevent action; and

(c) the issuance of false and misleading statements concerning the "action" which they have taken to date.

. . . While the State Department has been thus "exploring" the whole refugee problem, without distinguishing between those who are in imminent danger of death and those who are not, hundreds of thousands of Jews have been allowed to perish.

*(Treasury Secretary Morganthau concluded his Personal Report to the President as follows:)*

. . . The facts I have detailed in this report, Mr. President, came to the Treasury's attention as a part of our routine investigation of the licensing of the financial phases of the proposal of the World Jewish Congress for the evacuation of Jews from France and Rumania. The facts may thus be said to have come to light through accident. How many others of the same character are buried in State Department files is a matter I would have no way of knowing. . . . This much is certain, however. The matter of rescuing the Jews from extermination is a trust too great to remain in the hands of men who are indifferent, callous and perhaps even hostile. The task is filled with difficulties. Only a fervent will to accomplish, backed by persistent and untiring effort, can succeed where time is so precious.

---

8. On March 24, 1944, President Roosevelt issued a strong accusation and warning which was published widely in Allied and neutral nations and air-dropped in leaflet form by the millions over Nazi-occupied territories. Finally the President had become convinced of the facts concerning Hitler's war against the Jews. Now he acted forcefully, but too late to save the millions who had already gone to their deaths.

In one of the blackest crimes of all history—begun by the Nazis in the day of peace and multiplied by them a hundred times in time of war—the wholesale systematic murder of the Jews of Europe goes on unabated every hour. . . . That these innocent people, who have already survived a decade of Hitler's fury, should perish on the very eve of triumph over the barbarism which their persecution symbolizes, would be a major tragedy.

PRESIDENTIAL STATEMENT, MARCH 24, 1944 (ON THE DESTRUCTION OF EUROPEAN JEWRY)

It is therefore fitting that we should again proclaim our

determination that none who participate in these acts of savagery shall go unpunished. . . . That warning applies not only to the leaders but also to their functionaries and subordinates in Germany and in the satellite countries. All who knowingly take part in the deportation of Jews to their death in Poland or Norwegians and French to their death in Germany are equally guilty with the executioner. All who share the guilt shall share the punishment.

Hitler is committing these crimes against humanity in the name of the German people. I ask every German and every man everywhere under Nazi domination to show the world by his action that in his heart he does not share these insane criminal desires. Let him hide these pursued victims, help them to get over their borders, and do what he can to save them from the Nazi hangman. I ask him also to keep watch, and to record the evidence that will one day be used to convict the guilty.

# PART TWO

# THE HOLOCAUST

Yellow stars,
mass produced,
were later cut
from large pieces
of fabric. All
Jews wore a star
on their clothes.

# CHAPTER ELEVEN

# THE JEWS IN GERMANY

(Facing page): The family of Max Pinkus around 1910-14. This family of industrialists lived in Silesia, then part of Germany. They owned textile mills and estates and were patrons of the arts. There were many well-to-do Jewish families in Germany as well as middle-class families of businessmen, doctors, and other professionals.

Soon after the National Socialists came to power in 1933, the noted German teacher, scholar, and rabbi, Leo Baeck, told a group of Jewish leaders: "The thousand-year history of the German Jews has come to an end." Baeck's words were prophetic, but most German Jews rejected them. Instead, they believed that the Nazis were merely the most recent in a long history of anti-Semitic persecutors who had always come and gone. The German Jews had learned to live with anti-Semitism in the long run and to combat it in the short run.

This meant fighting anti-Semitism as best they could. In 1893, the Central Association of German Citizens of Jewish Faith was founded to publicize Jewish contributions to German civilization and culture, and to refute the lies of anti-Semites. Beginning in 1929, when National Socialist victories threatened the republic, the Central Association became more aggressive. Together with the Zionist Federation of Germany and in alliance with liberal and moderate political parties, it worked to pressure government officials away from anti-Semitic stands. These tactics showed the organized German Jewish community to be the most important force in Germany working against the rise of the Nazis. But the general population was unwilling or unable to resist Hitler, and the best Jews could do was to hold on and hold out, bargain and negotiate. This was the strategy which appealed to most Jews during the first two years of the National Socialist regime.

A synagogue in the Jewish quarter of Berlin.

The five hundred thousand Jews of Germany had much in common. Well over eighty percent were natives, and about as many affiliated with the liberal wing of Judaism, which was similar to the Conservative movement in America. Most lived in big cities and were business or professional people, and most of these were self-employed. The Jews of each city were members of a *Gemeinde*, a communal religious organization of which there were over thirteen hundred. Supported by state taxes on Jews, these public bodies maintained synagogues, promoted religious education, and dispensed charity. The Gemeinden of each state belonged to a central association.

The largest secular organization of German Jewry was the Central Association, whose membership in 1933 was seventy thousand families. The Zionist Federation of Germany, by contrast, had only ten thousand members. The Central Association rejected the Zionist commitment to Palestine as the Jewish national home, but it generally supported practical efforts to build Palestine as a place of refuge for Jews. The more conservative Federal Union of Jewish War Veterans, whose thirty thousand members tended to be single-minded German patriots, was constantly and strongly anti-Zionist.

The average German Jew, then, was native, metropolitan, in business or a profession, centrist in politics, and more passionately attached to Germany than to Jewishness. In contrast to this model were three minority groups—the Orthodox, the Zionists, and the East European Jews. The Orthodox, about fifteen percent of the population, were unique in their primary attachment to Judaism. They were represented by Agudat Israel, an organization which stood for the preservation of Torah within the world of modern secular culture. But even the Orthodox had deep roots in Germany, and their patriotism was sincere and meaningful. The Zionists and East European Jews, on the other hand, challenged the idea that Jews "belonged" in Germany. As a result, most German Jews felt socially and politically distant from these groups, which represented some twenty percent of the community. Even further on the conservative and liberal fringes of German Jewry were small numbers of very nationalist and Communist individuals.

The Nazi rise to power sent shock waves throughout the Jewish population from right to left: on the other hand, panic and flight, despair and suicide; on the other, steadfastness and solidarity, courage and a stubborn will to resist. Immediately after Hitler was appointed Chancellor, the Central Association issued a defiant public statement: "We are convinced that no one will dare to violate our constitutional rights. Every adverse attempt will find us at our post ready for resolute defense." Jews were advised, "Stand by calmly."

In a matter of days and weeks, the worst predictions about the Nazis became realities. Thousands upon thousands of Jews lost their jobs, and hundreds of Jewish communities were terrorized. Some Jews who before had believed so deeply in Germany now, in despair, committed suicide. Many more, some thirty-seven thousand in 1933 alone, fled the country. Most of those who left hoped and believed that their departure would be temporary, that the Nazi regime would soon collapse. Most German Jews still resoundingly affirmed the right of Jews to be German, to live in and love Germany. All Jewish organizations—from Orthodox to Reform, conservative to liberal, Zionist to non-Zionist—still believed that maintaining a Jewish presence in Germany was a legal right, a moral necessity, and a religious commandment.

The Central Association, on March 9, 1933, proclaimed that: "Germany will remain Germany and no one can rob us of our homeland and our fatherland." A vice-president of the association offered a message of faith and hope in a German future for the Jews:

Leo Baeck,
1873-1956.

*Fear? We have shown by a thousand martyrs that we have no fear of the deeds of human beings. Desperation? Even in the most trying times Jewry has never been desperate but was always strengthened by its faith in God and by the consciousness of its right. Faith? Yes. Faith in the inner strength which is born of the knowledge of events, and a clear conscience. Hope? Yes. The hope that coexistence through centuries with the German people will prove itself stronger than all prejudices.*

Even the Zionist groups admitted the strong influence of Germany on the Jews. "The historical tie of centuries is not so easy to dissolve," read one editorial. Even those Jews who left Germany took much with them: "Generations will remain faithful to what they received from the German spirit." Similar sentiments were even more strongly expressed, of course, by Reform and anti-Zionist leaders. After the war, survivors would grieve at not having advised those hundreds of thousands who were later murdered to flee right away at all costs.

Ironically, for most German Jews, the first response to National Socialism was to blame themselves. The Orthodox accepted the ancient formula which interpreted persecution as resulting from sin. God, they believed, was using the Nazis to warn Jews to repent, to return to their faith. Similarly, Zionists argued that Jews were to blame because they had been ashamed or embarrassed to be themselves. "Wear the Yellow Badge with Pride," an editorial proclaimed.

*Jewry bears a great guilt because it failed to heed Theodor Herzl's call and even mocked it in some instances. The Jews refused to acknowledge that "the Jewish question still exists." They thought the only important thing was not to be recognized as Jews. Today we are being reproached with having betrayed the German people; the National Socialist press calls us the "enemies of the nation," and there is nothing we can do about it. It is not true that the Jews have betrayed Germany. If they have betrayed anything, they have betrayed themselves and Judaism.*

*Because the Jews did not display their Jewishness with pride, because they wanted to shirk the Jewish question, they must share the blame for the degradation of Jewry.*

Many Jews looked to their religion and their community for comfort. Rabbi Baeck urged them to discover themselves and renew their history. Perhaps even more persuasive in summoning his fellow Jews to Jewish self-awareness was the scholar Martin Buber. His books and lectures stirred German Jews to be true to Jewish values and spirit in the totality of their lives.

The synagogues became full to overflowing. They were not only houses of prayer, but also places of solidarity and caring which defied the loneliness outside. People who had never been in a synagogue before came to pray or, at the very least, to be with other Jews. Judaism flowered during those early years of National Socialism as a spontaneous response to persecution.

As always in hard times, the cycle of Jewish festivals gained freshness and relevance. Passover, the festival of freedom, became a living reality. At Purim, during the reading of the Scroll of Esther, Haman became Hitler and noisemaking drowned out his name. Hanukkah, once little more than a substitute for Christmas in Germany, now was restored to commemoration of the Maccabean struggle for freedom against the pagans. The Hanukkah Haftarah took on new meaning: "Not by might, nor by power, but by My spirit, says the Lord of hosts."

---

**Kiddush Hashem or Suicide?**   To imagine that the Jews walked willingly to their deaths during the Holocaust is to accuse them of committing suicide. Nothing could be farther from the way of life commanded the Jew by tradition. Jewish tradition makes a sharp distinction between suicide and martyrdom. Taking one's own life when not under duress is regarded as a terrible act, an insult to God in whose image the human being is created. It can only be viewed by the Jew as a result of mental illness and loss of judgment.

In the early centuries of the Diaspora, there was little discussion of this problem. But in the years of the Crusades the Jews were persecuted so fiercely that many committed suicide rather than fall prey to the zealous Christian armies crossing Europe. This gave rise to much discussion of the problem among Jewish authorities, who reaffirmed that suicide was unacceptable except in the most extreme cases.

Recently, Chief Rabbi Goren of the Israel Defense Forces wrote that captured Jewish soldiers should be permitted to decide whether their particular situation warranted suicide. But the thought of suicide is so foreign to the Jewish tradition that this ruling has been criticized by many other Jewish authorities.

**Faith and Doubt**   Jewish Law is mainly concerned with the way in which people act, not in what they believe. Some scholars have argued that Judaism is a system of law above all else. But the commandments of the Bible and the demands made in rabbinic literature are based on

102

the assumption that people must have trust and confidence that God cares about what human beings do. Jewish faith maintains that God reveals truth to us in order that we will be able to choose between what is right and what is wrong. We must have faith in God (Proverbs 28:20) because God has faith in us (Deuteronomy 32:4).

Often, though, as in the Book of Job, our faith is challenged. After the Holocaust, many philosophers, Jewish and non-Jewish, inquired seriously, "Where was God?" It is remarkable, reading the surviving records of the Holocaust victims, that this attitude of doubt was foreign to them. They recited the hymn, *Ani Ma 'amin*, "I believe with perfect faith . . .," even in the face of death.

# CHAPTER TWELVE

# FROM FREEDOM TO GHETTO

A Jewish conference, with both reformers and Zionists in attendance, happened to be meeting when the news became known that Hitler had been named Chancellor. On that day, January 30, 1933, the chairman told his colleagues: "A historical turning point has been reached. All differences among Jews have now become meaningless. We are all in the same danger." Actually, both the Gemeinden and the national organizations, like the Central Association and B'nai B'rith, had already been working for months on a defense plan to unify the Jewish community.

Yet the various factions and parties within the community were unable to come together in one effective central body before Hitler came to power. By April 1933, the best they could do was agree to the founding of a Central Committee of German Jews for Relief and Reconstruction. While this agency provided a way to channel desperately needed welfare funds from abroad for the mammoth tasks of welfare facing German Jewry, leaders like Leo Baeck and Martin Buber actively sought a more influential political representative body.

By the fall of 1933, the Federal Representation of German Jews was founded to provide for Jewish solidarity, and this it did to a limited extent. Both Orthodox and Zionist groups believed that the Federal Representation was inadequate and unbalanced. Indeed, its published goal of creating "a vigorous and honorable Jewish life on German soil within the German state" was something no one knew how to achieve. At best, memoranda and petitions could be sent to try to

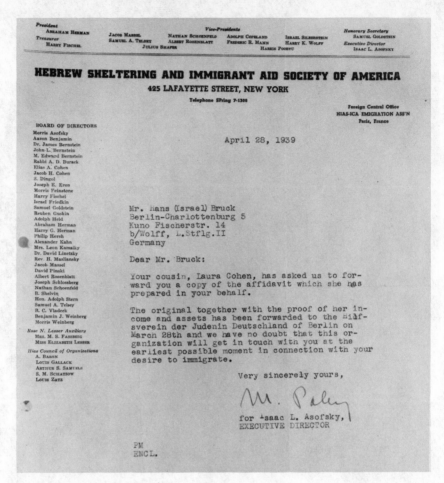

## HEBREW SHELTERING AND IMMIGRANT AID SOCIETY OF AMERICA

### 425 LAFAYETTE STREET, NEW YORK

Telephone SPring 7-1360

Foreign Central Office
HIAS-ICA EMIGRATION ASS'N
Paris, France

April 28, 1939

Mr. Hans (Israel) Bruck
Berlin-Charlottenburg 5
Kuno Fischerstr. 14
b/Wolff, L.Stflg.II
Germany

Dear Mr. Bruck:

Your cousin, Laura Cohen, has asked us to forward you a copy of the affidavit which she has prepared in your behalf.

The original together with the proof of her income and assets has been forwarded to the Hilfsverein der Judenin Deutschland of Berlin on March 28th and we have no doubt that this organization will get in touch with you at the earliest possible moment in connection with your desire to immigrate.

Very sincerely yours,

for Isaac L. Asofsky,
EXECUTIVE DIRECTOR

PM
ENCL.

save Jews from "protective custody," violence, and brutality.

In general, all Jewish organizations were forced to accommodate the National Socialist regime. When the first vote of public confidence for Hitler was taken in November 1933, the Federal Representation recommended to the German Jews that they, too, were required to support the regime:

> *With the entire German people also we Jews as citizens are summoned to cast our votes on the foreign policy of the Reich government. They are required for Germany's equality among the nations, the conciliation of the nations, and for the peace of the world. Despite all that we have had to undergo;*
> *The vote of the German Jews can be only Yes.*

Just a few months before, the Zionists had made various proposals to the government, and they took that opportunity to state an official position:

> *On the foundations of the new state, which has established the principle of race, we wish so to fit in our community into the total structure that for us too, in the sphere assigned to us, fruitful activity for the Fatherland is possible.*

Both Zionists and non-Zionists proposed that the Jewish community should sponsor programs for job retraining so that Jews would be able to fill jobs more "useful" than the ones they were losing because of anti-Semitic discrimination. These groups also petitioned, in vain, for government support of emigrants and controls against anti-Semitism.

No response was ever received from the authorities, and it became clear that the Federal Representation had little power as a spokesman for German Jewry. But it did serve as a sort of self-government which took on enormous responsibilities within the Jewish community. It supplied the worldwide press with proof of the terror facing German Jews. It tried to save Jewish property and funds from the Nazis. It even kept a university running by telling the government that it was only an institution to train rabbis and teachers of Jewish religion. This university was an important asset in these times when Jews were barred from German universities, and when the government expelled Jewish children from elementary and high schools, the Federal Representation began to run a successful network of private Jewish schools.

As early as May 1933, Martin Buber proposed that schools run by the Jewish community should "not merely remedy an external state of distress, but should also fill a great internal void . . . by providing our youth with the firm stability of being united with the eternity of Judaism." The Federal Representation agreed, and it issued guidelines for schools to teach about the contributions of Jews and Judaism to Germany as well as those of German culture to the Jews. In practice, some teachers were more interested in educating pupils to be Zionists, speak Hebrew, and understand Jewish history; others neglected these subjects and taught as if they were in German public schools where Jewish matters were of little importance. But despite the tensions created by both students and teachers who were unprepared for this new situation, the Jewish school offered the Jewish

EDUCATION AND EMIGRATION

child shelter from the storm outside, warmth and love instead of rejection and hostility, and new self-esteem.

Adult Jewish education also progressed remarkably through the growth of the Frankfurt *Lehrhaus* founded in 1920, and in other programs organized by the new Central Office of Jewish Adult Education established in 1934 by the Federal Representation. With Martin Buber in the lead, lectures, discussions, courses, and even community singing were begun. Subjects studied included Bible, history, philosophy, and languages—English, Spanish, and Hebrew were most useful for future emigrants. All these efforts gave spiritual life to the community, but many Jews unfortunately tricked themselves into believing "that we had very, very much time."

Some individual Jews did decide to emigrate. In years of repression like 1933, there were many, but in calmer times the rate slowed to about twenty-three thousand per year. Everyone would speculate on the direction in which government policies might lead. Even Leo Baeck dreamed that Hitler would soon be overthrown and that people would wake up one day and find billboards announcing a military take-over.

The major difficulty was finding a place to go. Visas, work permits, and other necessary papers were hard to acquire, and most of those available were for countries in Central and South America, which were too hazardous for elderly immigrants. Many German Jews were troubled by the thought of leaving Germany to go to a place with few existing Jewish institutions, a place where it would be difficult to find kosher food, synagogues, Jewish cemeteries, and ritual baths. Staying in Germany may have seemed a smaller risk.

Immigration to Palestine was tightly controlled. Not only did the British restrict the number of permits, but the Zionist movement itself set rigid standards for prospective immigrants. The needs and interests of Palestine for young, healthy people and those with appropriate work skills and/or money to invest sometimes conflicted with the strategies of rescue. Only after "the night of shattered glass" in 1938 did the Zionists push to bring in masses of German Jews, often illegally.

The German Jewish community was rapidly aging, and younger persons emigrated in the greatest percentages, since they could most easily try for a fresh start in a new home. The American Jewish leaders worried that Germany was becoming a gigantic old-age home which would eventually need total support from foreign Jewish charity. Between January 1933 and November 1938, some one

Many immigrant
ships brought
refugees from
Europe to safety
in Palestine.

hundred fifty thousand Jews—thirty percent of the original population—left Germany. After "the night of shattered glass," under Nazi
pressure, nearly another one hundred fifty thousand left.

**T**he National Socialist victory in 1933 had shaken the Jewish community, but in a few short months it rallied with energy and will for unity and a positive commitment to Jewish identity. There was hope, faith, and belief that the German dictatorship would soon fall, or at the very least would tolerate Jewish life. After the Nuremberg Laws were adopted in 1935, this hope diminished and began to disappear.

Jewish organizations had to conduct their business in the presence of Gestapo agents, and rabbis had to fear that they would be summoned for questioning if they said anything critical of government policies. Buber was banned from public speaking. Baeck was arrested again and again. He wrote a prayer to be read at Kol Nidre services, and the Nazis discovered it, arrested him, and suppressed the text, which began this way:

> *In this hour every man in Israel stands erect before his Lord, the God of justice and mercy, to open his heart in prayer. Before God we will question our ways and search our deeds, the acts we have done and those we have left undone. We will publicly confess the sins we have committed and beg the Lord to pardon and forgive. Acknowledging our trespasses, individual and communal, let us despise the slanders and calumnies directed against us and our faith. Let us declare them lies, too mean and senseless for our reckoning.*
>
> *God is our refuge. Let us trust Him our source of dignity and pride. Thank the Lord and praise Him for our destiny, for the honor and persistence with which we have endured and survived persecution.*

German Jewry had once been a prosperous community, contributing generously toward the needs of less fortunate Jews around the world. By 1936, twenty percent were living in poverty. Jewish public kitchens dispensed 2,357,000 free meals that year, and more than 75,000 persons received free matzot during Passover. By January 1938, one leader publicly declared: "To those among our youth who have not yet decided to emigrate, I say, there is no future for Jews in this country. Whatever chances may be forthcoming for us will probably not be for the better." Fourteen months later, Martin Buber wrote that the creative living together and sharing of Germans and Jews was doomed. "I testify: it was the most extraordinary and meaningful circumstance. . . . But . . . [it] is at an end and it is not likely to return."

**The Search for Knowledge**   The Jewish commitment to pursuit of God's truth makes education a prime value. The entire Book of Proverbs is a hymn to wisdom, the beginning of which is reverence for God (Proverbs 1:7). Since the Bible demands that families educate their young (Deuteronomy 6:7), the Land of Israel was noted in ancient times for one of the earliest public school systems in the world (Baba Batra 21a; Josephus). Thus it was natural throughout the ages that even in the worst of situations Jewish communities would devote whatever resources were available to the support of Jewish learning. In modern times, Jews excelled in all areas of education—arts, sciences, languages, and mathematics—despite severe disadvantages which were placed on them by many majority cultures. The world suffered tragically because so many Jewish intellectuals were unable to escape Hitler's death camps. Fortunately, some, like Sigmund Freud and Albert Einstein, were able to flee. Even in the death camps themselves classes were conducted for the young, and discussion groups were held so that adults could continue their studies. Jewish historians wrote minutely detailed accounts of the Holocaust even as they were themselves caught in it, and Jewish scientists studied the behavior of their fellow inmates in the camps.

**A Jewish View of Charity**   The Hebrew word *tzedakah*, which is often translated as "charity," really means "justice." Jews believe that helping the poor and the needy is more than a nice voluntary act; rather, it is a commandment already found in the Torah (Deuteronomy 15:9-11). For example, in the rural, agricultural society of biblical times, farmers were required to leave a corner of their field unharvested so the poor might come and cut it and have food (Leviticus 19:9-10), and regular tithes were set aside for the benefit of widows, orphans, and the poor (Deuteronomy 14:28f). Besides giving generous support to the State of Israel, Jews in America today regularly make large donations to non-Jewish charities. Indeed, the tradition of Jewish charity is a cornerstone of American Jewish life.

# CHAPTER THIRTEEN

# DEATH AND LIFE IN THE EAST EUROPEAN GHETTOS

(Facing page): German soldiers mock and torture a barefoot Jew. He was probably forced to put on the *tallit* (prayer shawl) and *tefillin* (phylacteries). Note the slain bodies alongside him.

With the German invasion of Poland in September 1939, some two million Jews came under German rule. Two years later, when Hitler attacked the Soviet Union, some three million more Jews came under Nazi control. This massive Jewish community was highly concentrated: three hundred fifty thousand Jews in Warsaw equalled the entire Jewish population of France; and Lodz and Kiev had two hundred thousand and one hundred fifty thousand Jews respectively. In the past, the size and density of these Jewish communities enriched their creativity. Under the Nazis it would hasten their doom.

The Jews of Eastern Europe remembered World War I, and they knew that besides the common hardships of war they could expect bloody pogroms by the Germans and even by the Poles with whom they had lived for centuries in a state of tension. Tens of thousands of Jews were killed, wounded, or left homeless by the bombing and shelling during the German invasion. In Warsaw alone, about one-third of Jewish-owned buildings were demolished.

Tens of thousands of Jews fled eastward toward Russia, and as the German army advanced, even more were expelled. On foot, on carts, in wagons they set out with the few belongings they were able to save. Within a few months, thousands of Jewish settlements were erased from maps of Poland. Over three hundred thousand Polish Jews had become homeless refugees, beggars for bread and shelter, candidates for disease.

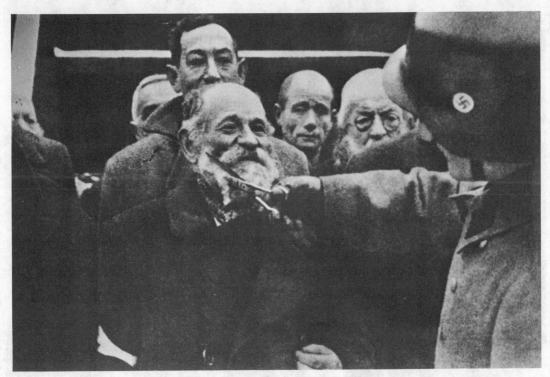

German soldiers amuse themselves by cutting the beards of Orthodox Jews.

As soon as the Germans entered a town or city, they turned the Jews into outcasts. They forced Jews out of soup lines and convinced Poles to do the same by explaining that more soup would then be left for Poles. Jewish stores were confiscated or plundered, and individuals were forced to give up all their possessions as well as large sums of money. Sometimes the SS would blackmail the community to cooperate by taking hostages, many of whom were never returned.

Killing and senseless violence became daily rituals. All over Poland synagogues went up in flames. Everywhere the Germans organized programs, rounding up the non-Jewish population to witness and learn how to abuse, injure, and murder Jews. In the territory taken from Russia in 1941, mass executions commonly destroyed thousands of Jews at once. Reports of the violence stunned and shocked the Jews. In one place, thousands of half-naked men and women were beaten to bleeding in the town square, then kept standing for hours in the biting frost. In another, the Germans arrested a beloved rabbi, tortured him, and savagely displayed his head for several days in the window of a main-street store.

The Germans took particular pleasure in being cruel to traditional Jews wearing hats and long coats, beard and sidelocks. Countless "games" involved forcing these Jews to eat pork, or setting their beards on fire. And German terror was used not only in "play," but also in forcing Jews to work. Often Jews were seized off the streets and even from their homes for forced labor. Sometimes they were released at the day's end, but more likely they were held for a week or two, unable to inform their families of their whereabouts or even that they were alive.

In time, the SS was operating some 125 forced labor camps just for Jews. Workers were commonly shot or beaten to death, and many more died of exhaustion or hunger. Underclothed and underfed, they suffered frostbite in the winter and sunburn in the summer. All sorts of diseases plagued them, yet they were expected to work as many as fourteen hours a day, walk miles to and from work, sleep out of doors, and survive on bits of bread and soup.

---

Throughout Poland, the Germans began to experiment with ghettos. In the spring of 1940, one hundred sixty thousand Jews in Lodz were sealed off, and in November nearly half a million were locked within walls and guarded gates in Warsaw. Large signs the Jews were forced to post there read "Danger: Epidemic Zone." The Cracow ghetto was enclosed within walls in the form of Jewish tombstones, symbols which were terrifyingly real. THE NAZI GHETTOS

The Jewish historian Emanuel Ringelblum wrote in his diary on November 8, 1940: "We are returning to the Middle Ages." Actually, the situation was much worse. In the Middle Ages, Jews had used the ghetto walls to survive the attacks of Crusaders. The ghetto also allowed Jews easy access to synagogues and other central institutions. Later, the church advocated separation of Christians and Jews, and the voluntary ghetto became obligatory. Although Jews had to wear badges and could not pursue certain occupations, the ghetto was not a prison. During the day, Jews were allowed to leave and Christians often entered to do business. By contrast, the Nazi ghetto was very much like the Nazi concentration camp—full of disease, forced labor, and death. Everyone felt this loss of human rights and dignity. A thirteen-year-old boy recorded in his diary the events of September 6, 1941, moving day into the Vilna ghetto: "I feel that I have been robbed, my freedom is being robbed from me, and my home, and the familiar Vilna streets I love so much."

The isolation was increased when all telephones were removed from private homes. (Radios had long since been confiscated.) Mail was censored and controlled, and parcels of food and clothing rarely escaped seizure by the Germans before they even reached the ghetto post office. Even the landscape heightened the somber sense of loneliness. In Warsaw, the Jewish quarter was reshaped to exclude its only park, and in Vilna just one tree grew in the ghetto. A popular song lamented: "For them the square and boulevards, for me a place of misery."

The ghettos were in the oldest, most run-down parts of town, often lacking basic necessities like proper lighting, paved streets, and sanitation facilities. The air was foul and the streets filthy. A doctor in Vilna wrote: "About twenty-five thousand persons live in our ghetto, in seventy-two buildings on five street sections. Comes to 1½-2 meters per person, narrow as a grave." Privacy, modesty, peace, and quiet were things of the past.

From the Warsaw ghetto a girl wrote:

> *My ears are filled with the deafening clamor of crowded streets and cries of people dying on the sidewalks. Even the quiet hours of the night are filled with the snoring and coughing of those who share the same apartment or, only too often, with the shots and screams coming from the streets!*

Staying warm became more important than cleanliness. In Warsaw, fuel was so scarce that coal was called "black pearls." Uninhabited buildings, stores, and fences soon were dismantled to provide wood for fuel. In the winter of 1941, the Germans confiscated what furs—coats, linings, collars, cuffs, skins—they could take from Polish Jews. That same winter, Ringelblum wrote in his diary, "The most fearful sight is that of freezing children, dumbly weeping in the street with bare feet, bare knees, and torn clothing."

---

THE
STARVATION
STRATEGY

**G**erman policy was to starve the Jews, since they were "a population which does no work worth mentioning." The rations for the ghetto included no meat, only bread and potatoes. These were often spoiled, stolen, or sold on the black market. Hunger was so bad that even potato peelings became normal food. Potatoes, one man wrote, are "our whole life. When I am alone in my room for a few moments of quiet, the echo of that word continues in my ears. Even in my dreams it visits me." Hunger overwhelmed everyone, but some faced their struggle heroically. One eleven-year-old girl posed as a model in her art class, and the other students gave her some small pieces of bread. She ate only a tiny piece, wrapping the rest in a bit of newspaper: "This will be for my little brother."

Only illegal smuggling of food into the ghettos kept most Jews from dying of hunger. Children were the most numerous class of smugglers, small, spry, and if caught, an object of pity for the police. Through the cleverness and daring, whole cows were transported from a Catholic cemetery to the ghetto in hearses; and small cranes, pipes, and troughs brought grain, milk, and vegetables from the "Aryan" side past the ghetto walls. Paradoxically, thievery and sneaking became prestigious kinds of work.

Hunger killed, but first it disabled peoples' bodies and minds. Fatigue, dizziness, nausea, vomiting, and diarrhea were daily complaints from the hungry of all ages. All forms of disease struck the ghetto and killed tens of thousands, particularly infants and the elderly. In January 1942, a welfare report summarized the conditions of the refugees in the Warsaw ghetto: "Hunger, sickness, and want are their constant companions, and death is the only visitor in their homes."

---

In the ghetto, the commonness of death heightened the value of life. Throughout their long history of being persecuted, the Jewish people held to a religious tradition which sanctified the preservation of life. Folk wisdom taught: "A Jew lives with hope." In Vilna, a popular ghetto song cried out:

MOSHE, HOLD ON

> *Moshe, hold on,*
> *Keep hold of yourself,*
> *Remember we must get out. . . .*
>
> *Moshe, hold on; hold on, Moshe —*
> *It isn't very long,*
> *The hour soon will toll. . . .*

The only gladdening aspect of the ghetto, one leader noted, was that Jews "fight so stubbornly for life." The community worked to keep despair away, and the rate of suicide remained quite low for this reason. In Warsaw, Jews turned political prophecy into a jingle:

> Listen here, Haman you,
> Jews will live to settle scores.
> You will get your comeuppance.
> Jews have lived and will endure,
> But Haman, you will go to hell.

In Vilna, a popular song urged:

> Let's be joyous and tell our jokes,
> We'll hold a wake when Hitler chokes.

The ghetto Jews realized that they had no choice but to come to terms with the days ahead in their prison. "Be pliable like a reed, not rigid like a cedar," the Talmud says. So Jews learned to compromise, innovate, and cleverly to survive. Not even threats of severe penalties kept them from violating curfew, smuggling, and leaving the ghetto illegally without wearing arm bands.

Family solidarity extended to embrace grandparents, aunts and uncles, married brothers and sisters. All pitched in to struggle for survival. Divorces ceased, and all ghettos recorded many marriages. Tenderness and affection, daring and heroism were the norms in the emotion-charged atmosphere. And most Jews felt a strong sense of belonging and a pride in their Jewish identity. In the Lodz ghetto, children presented a Hanukkah program in their school auditorium:

> Hunger, cold, and conflicts were forgotten. Shoemakers and tailors, physicians, lawyers, and pharmacists, all at once, we were one big family. That could not have happened in Berlin . . . but here, behind the barbed wire, something existed that united us all—our Jewishness. When they sang together, they forgot their suffering and misery; they were still alive and in song they praised God, who many times before had performed miracles. When they sang about the little lamp whose oil for one day lasted eight, the singers regained their courage and hope.

This was their faith: "Our existence as a people will not be destroyed. Individuals will be destroyed, but the Jewish community will live on."

**The Value of Freedom**   One of the central events of Jewish history was the passage of the Jews from Egypt to the Promised Land. It was not only a physical exodus, but also a journey from slavery to freedom. The morning blessings of the Jewish prayerbook include a benediction thanking God for making the worshipper a free person. And in the light of history, all Jews believe that people must be free in order that they can serve the one, all-important master, God. The Bible, written at a time when slave-holding was a commonly accepted business practice, carefully restricts treatment of slaves and makes clear that slavery is not a desirable practice. Unique among ancient law codes, the Bible demands punishment for masters who kill their slaves (Exodus 21:20), and it sets aside the fiftieth year as a Jubilee Year in which all slaves automatically become free (Leviticus 25:10). The rabbis of the Talmud added that slaves should have living conditions—food, drink, and sleep—equal to those of their masters (Kiddushin 20a). Freedom was so precious that the defenders of Masada took their own lives because they wished for no person, particularly the Roman emperor, to be their master (Josephus).

**If There is no Flour, There is no Torah**   One of the earliest prayers still in use today is the *Birkat Hamazon,* the blessing said after eating. The Jews have long recognized that food is basic to life and even in times of plenty they have not taken sustenance for granted. The Bible commands that one bless God after partaking of a meal, for it is through God's infinite goodness that creation sustains us (Deuteronomy 9:10). The ancient rabbis pointed out that where poverty and famine exist, there is no time for people to study—all their time is taken up in finding food enough to eat. "If there is no flour, there is no Torah" (Avot 3:21) became a basic Jewish dictum. It was one of the great miracles of the Holocaust that Jews deprived of sustenance were able to find strength in one another.

# CHAPTER FOURTEEN

# THE OFFICIAL COMMUNITY: THE JUDENRAT

**(Facing page) The first interrogation by the SS in the offices of the Warsaw Jewish Community.**

Upon entering Poland in 1939 and Russia in 1941, the German invaders ordered Jewish communal leaders to establish Jewish councils, *Judenräte*. This replaced the religious community structures called *kehillot* (congregations), which like all similar bodies had been shattered by the invasion, bombings, mass flights and evacuations, and most of all the ongoing German terror. By Nazi decree, communities with up to ten thousand inhabitants were to have a council of twelve members; large communities, twenty-four members.

Many reached their leadership positions in the usual ways: family prestige, wealth, Jewish learning, and dedication to the community through financial generosity and good works. Since World War I, activity in political parties or a social service profession was another way to become a community leader. As a group, these were decent, honest people, who served their fellow Jews in the spirit of the Talmudic saying, "Do not withdraw from the community." To be sure, some were tempted by the rewards of prestige and honor, but most regarded communal service as an obligation and responsibility.

No one could be sure exactly how the Judenräte would function. Though the Germans wanted these councils formed to carry out their orders, most Jews, leaders and masses alike, believed that the Judenräte would first and foremost represent Jewish needs to the Nazis. Thus the Jews in Eastern Europe actually wanted the Judenräte just as German Jewry was motivated to create the Federal Representa-

tion. They desired an official body to plead and negotiate with the authorities, hopefully to ward off any danger. Of course, some Jews were uncertain of this strategy, fearing that the Judenräte might well become another instrument of Nazi oppression.

Those who agreed to serve on the Judenräte usually did so with serious misgivings. Was it wise to follow German orders and form a council? Who would be the best representatives? If we reject our responsibility, whom will the Germans appoint in our places? In most cities and towns, few volunteered for the job, and names often had to be chosen by lot. Sometimes, no one volunteered to serve, and the Germans themselves made random appointments.

The worst fears about participating in the Judenräte came true. From the start, every order the Germans issued was enforced with unending terror. Within days, or at most, weeks, hundreds of Judenräte members were taken hostage, arrested, sent to labor camps, shot or hanged. Hundreds more fled for their lives. Commonly, the Germans would accuse Judenräte members of not following orders, or of delaying. The Nazis frequently blackmailed communities for enormous sums of money, threatening to kill Judenräte members if the money could not be raised. Such threats were carried out, and it became clear that the Judenräte had no choice but to obey German orders.

---

TRYING THE
IMPOSSIBLE

From the beginning, the Judenräte had two roles—to meet German demands, and to serve Jewish needs. Long before the Nazis there had been a Jewish community organization in tsarist Russia, the *kehilla*, which had faced a similar dilemma. The kehilla was responsible for social welfare, education, and religion, but it also had to enforce repressive taxation, military drafting, and other anti-Jewish orders on behalf of the tsarist government. Now the Judenräte in the ghettos, under far worse conditions, had to serve the German oppressors, yet at the same time try to comfort the Jewish oppressed.

The first task was to feed the hungry and heal the sick. Every community organized public kitchens, "tea houses," first-aid stations, hospitals, dental clinics, public baths, and barber shops. Orphans, the elderly, and other homeless people were given shelter, and children's day-care centers were established. Unfortunately, needs were always greater than resources. Judenräte officials humbled themselves pleading for their fellow Jews to the German authorities. They petitioned for release of hostages, news about prisoners, decrease in numbers of those taken for forced labor, and cessation of harassment and violence. Occasionally the petititions succeeded, and the Germans would enlarge a ghetto by a street or two or lower taxes by a bit. Flattery sometimes softened the Nazis, but bribery was considered more effective. Some Judenräte even kept furniture, jewelry, and other items on supply in case bribes were needed in emergency situations. But more often than not the greed of the Germans swallowed up gifts without returning sufficient benefits to the Jews.

One of the major tasks for the Judenräte was to supply forced labor for the government. This burden fell most often on the poorest Jews, who could not afford to pay for substitutes. As more and more workers were required of them, the Judenräte became increasingly strict, since the ghetto would suffer even worse if workers could not be found. Thus Jewish authorities came into conflict with other Jews, who often ran and hid from assignments to labor camps. Jewish society was on a collision course to internal conflict.

**T**he most successful strategy the Judenräte tried was to use Jewish productivity to guarantee Jewish existence. The bombings, lootings, and effects of ghettoization had destroyed most Jewish businesses and industry, but Jews in the ghetto still had the ability and desire for work. If the Germans could be made to see Jewish labor as a valuable resource, perhaps the Jews would have a chance to live out the war.

**GHETTO INDUSTRY, JEWISH POLICE**

Thus in 1940 and 1941, Jewish industry came alive. In many cities, the Germans supplied raw materials for Jewish industries such as clothing factories, bakeries, and carpentry shops. The Germans gained the products of hundreds of Jewish factories, workshops, and warehouses, and the Judenräte earned substantial sums of tax money. However, many Jews resisted paying taxes even to the Jewish community, and the only way to enforce such taxes was through the Jewish police.

The Germans originally set up Jewish police forces to enforce traffic laws and maintain peace and order in the ghetto. Like the Judenräte, the Jewish police soon took on dual responsibilities—to protect the Jewish community, as well as to enforce German orders. Unlike the Judenräte members, though, those who joined the police did so voluntarily, often because they valued military-style life. Many were people who had converted from Judaism, but who were considered "racially" Jewish. Emanuel Ringelblum reported hearing one of these ex-Jews shout, "Down with the Jews!" inside one of the two Catholic churches which were within the Warsaw ghetto limits.

To be sure, many ghettos had police chiefs who were kind-hearted and community-minded. But they too, like Judenräte officials, lived under the threat of German terror. Supervised by Polish German guards, they had to be careful when checking people entering or leaving the ghetto. Once a Jewish woman brought into the Warsaw ghetto a sack of potatoes, which a German guard on duty immediately confiscated. A Jewish policeman asked the German to return the potatoes to the poor woman, and the angry guard knocked the policeman down, bayoneted him, and then shot him. Soon the soft-hearted were all but eliminated from the Jewish police, leaving mostly ruthless people who were willing to use clubs and rubber hoses to force their fellow Jews to obey the Germans. Instead of protecting the ghetto, the Jewish police often became its enemies.

---

JEWISH FRAUD

The Jews of Eastern Europe were not ready or able to govern themselves in the world created by the Nazi invasion. Few were trained civil servants, and many of the best leaders were either afraid to act effectively, or imprisoned, or murdered. The advantages of working for the Judenräte—higher pay, extra food rations, freedom from forced labor—drew into the bureaucracy many Jews who had only selfish motives. Connections became the route to preferred treatment, and soon much of Jewish life was determined by pull or protection, often called "Vitamin P."

Personal influence became very important in these horrible times, when hunger often broke down all rules of morality. Sometimes those with "Vitamin P" enjoyed benefits at the expense of others. But more frequently, there was simply not enough food, clothing, or shelter for anyone.

Those who suffered blamed not only the Germans, but also the Judenräte officials and the Jewish police. The Judenrat ("Jewish Board") became known as the "Jewish Fraud," and soon the Judenrat was seen as a mere tool of the Nazis. As the Judenräte ceased to be regarded as the authentic voice of the Jews in the ghettos, new organizations arose to challenge the Judenräte's authority. Some eventually formed an alternative community, others a countercommunity.

124

**The Problem of Leadership** Through the ages the Jewish community has developed a wide range of differing leaders, from prophets and
priests to kings, sages, and elders. Each person who assumed a
position of authority was expected to serve the community wisely and
selflessly, and so each leader was regarded as working not only for the
people but also for the sake of heaven. Rarely was this task as difficult
as during the Holocaust, for never before had the Jews been so helpless
in the grips of so ruthless an enemy.

Ancient pagan rulers and medieval Moslem and Christian
monarchs had usually allowed the Jews living under their power to
maintain limited self-government in return for heavy taxes and cooperation with civil laws. Hitler, on the other hand, forced Jews to set up
Judenräte in order to have them organize their own destruction. The
Final Solution presented impossible challenges to Jewish leaders, no
matter their ability. A few responded to the challenge in shameful
ways, but the majority still sought to serve the community "for the sake
of heaven."

**The Jews Under Duress** The Jewish idea that people should be
responsible for their actions is greatly threatened when individuals or
communities are subjected to severe pressures. In the one hundred
years leading up to the beginning of the Spanish Inquisition in 1480,
over one hundred thousand Jews were forced to practice their Judaism
secretly and at the risk of losing their lives. As late as the present
century, their descendants could be found in Spain and Portugal still
practicing Jewish rituals secretly, though no Inquisition threatened
them any longer. Such was the strength of their faith and the force of
their tradition.

Yet long centuries of persecution often kept Jews from living
up to traditional responsibilities required by the Torah. Medieval and
modern rabbinic authorities often discussed the problems of trying to
be Jewish during such periods as the Holocaust. In general, they
agreed the Torah mercifully exempts those under duress (Nedarim
27a; Baba Kamma 28b), and that God forgives even those Jews forced
to commit terrible sacrileges to escape torture or death.

# CHAPTER FIFTEEN

# THE ALTERNATIVE COMMUNITY: VOLUNTARY ORGANIZATIONS

**(Facing page) Soup kitchen in a Jewish orphans' home.**

Despite the attempts by the Germans to impose a state of barbarism upon them, the Jews worked persistently to maintain their organized society and culture. Despite the state of war and total insecurity, the Jews in nearly every ghetto defied the Germans by providing themselves with arts, literature, and society. The beautiful and meaningful aspects of human life never ceased in the Jewish community. The community was served by a wide range of institutions, for the traditional synagogue and ḥeder to modern social welfare organizations and cultural associations. Unlike the Judenräte, these groups were voluntary, self-supporting, and established solely for raising the level of Jewish life. Besides answering particular needs, the unofficial community institutions also strengthened the spirit of the ghetto, and gave a feeling of belonging and pride in times of deep despair and low morale.

The difficulties of wartime gave rise to several new Jewish self-help organizations. At first, Jews and Poles together planned city-wide blackout practices, civilian shelters, fire fighting, and first-aid services. Some months after the fall of Warsaw, in January 1940, the Germans ordered the Poles to split from the Jews, and Jewish Communal Self-Help became an independent association. Within a year, there were 118 local branches, and by 1942 there were 412. The aim was simple, according to founder Michal Weichert (1890–1967), teacher, lawyer, journalist, and actor before the war. A German officer once asked Weichert, "Don't you realize that you are on a sinking

ship?" "I know," he replied, "but I think that one must rescue people even from a sinking ship."

Funding for Jewish Communal Self-Help came largely from American Jews. The Joint Distribution Committee spent about $1 million a year in Poland until America's entry into the war, on December 7, 1941, halted the legal transfer of funds. Other support came from the German civil administration of Poland and from local Jewish contributions. Like the Judenräte, the Self-Help network provided food, child-care, and other forms of social welfare.

Relations between Self-Help branches and Judenräte were sometimes close and cooperative, but more often marked by tension and friction. There was frequent disagreement over strategies of community work, and at times the rivalry between organizations harmed community interests. Yet tens of thousands of families were aided by Jewish Communal Self-Help, which commonly organized small grass-roots committees representing even the poorest of tenement dwellers. The poor were asked to contribute a spoonful of flour or sugar toward a general collection to help those who were still poorer. Those who had nothing to give offered their labor. Young people provided the back-bone for the committees' daily tasks and special activities: caring for children in makeshift nurseries and classrooms, making the rounds for collections, organizing entertainment, and warning tenants about the arrival of the Jewish police or the SS. These committees protected the tenants, and they became the core of opposition to the Judenräte.

RELIGIOUS LIFE

Traditionally observant Jews accounted for a large segment of East European Jewry, despite the rise of more secular behavior, especially in the West. Jewish norms and values shaped community life, and nearly all Jews observed the Sabbath as a day of rest and abstained from non-kosher foods. Judaism was practiced in thousands of formal and informal settings; synagogues, study houses, *yeshivot* and *hedarim*, ritual baths, kosher slaughtering plants, religious courts, women's organizations, publishing houses and presses.

The Germans declared that Jews were a racial, not a religious group, so the observance of Judaism was for the most part outlawed. Those who continued in traditional practices were targeted for abuse and mockery by the Germans, and most synagogues were destroyed or desecrated, but most leaders of the religious community were able to function in secret. All through Poland, Jews prayed in

**A children's choir.**

hiding.

On August 12, 1940, on the eve of *Tisha B'Av*, the fast-day commemorating the destruction of the Temple, Chaim Kaplan noted: "Public prayer in these dangerous times is a forbidden act. Anyone caught in this crime is doomed to severe punishment. If you will, it is even sabotage and anyone engaging in sabotage is subject to execution." But Jews prayed in thousands of secret *minyanim*, some six hundred in Warsaw alone. They prayed in cellars, attics, back rooms, behind drawn blinds, with men on guard. In Cracow, services were held in two prayer houses thanks to the cooperation of Jewish policemen who worshipped there and who warned the congregation when German police were to be expected.

Prayer took on new seriousness and urgency. Passages written hundreds of years earlier during the Crusades were recited everyday instead of just on special occasions, since they now expressed immediate daily concerns. But many pious Jews had been shaken from their faith. In one Warsaw congregation, the news that the Jews would be confined in a ghetto arrived just as the cantor was about to start *Neilah*, the closing service of Yom Kippur, when worshippers ask God for salvation before the heavenly gates of mercy close. At once the cantor halted the service, saying that there was no point in praying when the gates of mercy were already locked.

Most observance of *kashrut* ceased, except among the most pious. Kosher meat was available only illegally, and therefore at great risk. At times of severe hunger, some rabbis even advised people to eat non-kosher food because they were in danger of starvation. Passover presented the most difficult problem, since the Nazis never permitted enough matzot to be baked. Beet juice, sweetened with saccharin, substituted for seder wine. "The only thing we had aplenty," said one Jew, "was bitter herbs—not on the table, but in our hearts."

Like kashrut and Passover, the Sabbath was nearly impossible to observe. The Germans deliberately forced Jews to sacrifice tradition by working on Saturdays, the High Holy Days and other festivals. Similar breaks with Judaism were necessitated because ritual baths were forbidden. In most cases, rabbis advised that saving a life was the highest value in Judaism, and that these were times when some compromises were necessary.

EDUCATION AND CULTURE

**W**hen the Germans entered Poland, they closed down the Jewish schools and ordered the public schools to exclude all Jewish pupils. The Germans intended to deprive Jewish children of education, but they underestimated the place of learning in the system of Jewish values. Within months of the German invasion, thousands of students were studying in several hundred ḥedarim across the country. General education flourished as well, since Jews were committed to modern secular studies as an important tool for participation in political, economic, and social life. Yet until the Germans finally agreed in October 1941—and then only in a limited way—to allow school for Jewish youngsters, all teaching had to take place in hiding.

*Jewish children learn in secret. In back rooms, on long benches near a table, little schoolchildren sit and learn what it's like to be Marranos. . . . In time of danger the children learn to hide their books. Jewish children are clever—when*

**A street singer.**

*they set off to acquire forbidden learning, they hide their
books and notebooks between their trousers and their
stomachs, then button their jackets and coats.*

Like the Jewish schools in Germany after 1933, the ghetto schools
formed a subcommunity of love and dedication that gave children
shelter, warmth, medical care, food, emotional security, and a sense of
Jewish identity and solidarity. Describing a high-school exhibit on
Yiddish literature, one poet wrote, "Death itself shrinks before this
beauty."

All forms of culture sustained life in the ghetto. Since curfew
rules did not allow people on the street from 7:00 P.M. until 5:00 A.M.
the next morning, socializing had to be among friends living the same
building or visitors who spent the night. Cardplaying was very popular,

and actors, musicians, comics, singers, and dancers all entertained small groups who came together for a few hours to forget their daily terror and despair.

Various groups tried to raise the level of cultural life in the ghetto and to give it particular Jewish flavor and meaning. The Yiddish Cultural Organization and *Tekumah* — a society for Hebrew culture — brought language and literature to many Jews who were able to attend scholarly lectures, courses, and special programs. The large ghettos had music too, especially orchestras which featured works by Jewish composers. And after the Germans shut down libraries and bookstores, several ghettos established underground libraries with daring couriers who delivered volumes in secret.

In these many ways, the Jews of the East European ghettos won a spiritual victory over the Nazis. The Jewish community organizations offered welfare, religious, educational, and cultural services which created a sense of normality and civilized dignity in times of barbarism and repression. Operating under terror, amid hunger and disease, they succeeded in helping those they reached to retain and enrich their Jewishness and their humanity.

---

ISSUES AND VALUES

**The Role of Community in Jewish Life**   When the Romans destroyed the Jewish state in the year 70, they did not destroy the Jewish community. Wherever Jews came to live in the Diaspora, they banded together to protect one another and promote the quality of Jewish life. Throughout the Middle Ages, each Jewish community, no matter what its size, undertook to provide its members with basic health care, education, and welfare services, fulfilling the rabbis' saying, "All Jews are responsible for one another" (Shevvot 39a). Particular duties were often taken up by organizations like the *Ḥevrah Kaddishah*, which cared for the dead and mourners, and the *Bikkur Ḥolim* societies, which visited and aided the sick. Memberships in groups like these was considered a high honor.

**Tisha B'Av**   Some of the most tragic events of Jewish history have coincidentally taken place on the ninth day of the Jewish month of Av (which falls in July or August). The First and Second Temples in Jerusalem were destroyed in 586 BCE and 70 CE, the second revolt against Rome was finally put down in the year 135, and the Jews were expelled from Spain in 1492 — all on the same calendar date, the ninth

132

of Av. In memoriam of these terrible events, synagogue worship on Tisha B'Av includes the reading of the Book of Lamentations and the recitation of *kinot*, קִינוֹת , dirges. A new memorial day, *Yom Hashoah*, יוֹם הַשׁוֹאָה , Holocaust Remembrance Day, was inaugurated by the Knesset of Israel in 1951. It falls on the twenty-seventh day of Nisan, between the anniversaries of the Warsaw Ghetto Uprising and the Israeli War of Independence. But even as Tisha B'Av took on new meaning for the Jews during the Holocaust years, so now the prayers recited on that day give us reason to recall the Holocaust.

# CHAPTER SIXTEEN

# THE COUNTER COMMUNITY: THE POLITICAL UNDERGROUND

**(Facing page) Smuggling food over the ghetto wall, Warsaw.**

Even before the rise of Hitler, European Jews never had very much political power. The Jewish community did have political life, however, which centered around active political parties. These parties all fought for equality and rights denied to Jews, and in doing so they instilled dignity and honor in the Jewish community. Each party, from Zionist to socialist, was committed to a certain political philosophy and program for the future, and each maintained a wide range of institutional activities, from schools and youth groups to women's organizations, cultural groups, charitable services, and publications.

The invasions of 1939 shattered this complex political system, just as they tore apart Jewish self-government. Party leaders and activists fled from the Nazis, who sought to arrest them and often killed them. Political parties were outlawed, and those activities which could be carried on in secret often had to be directed by young and inexperienced leaders. The biggest parties, like the General Zionists, lost many of their leaders to the Judenräte, and only the smaller liberal and radical groups of socialist Zionists and Jewish Communists were able to function effectively underground. Particularly active were the socialist Zionist youth movements, including *Dror, Hashomer Hatzair, Hehalutz,* and *Gordonia.*

**T**he ideas of socialism and Zionism were especially suited to these difficult times. For socialist and Zionist party insiders, these movements offered clear programs of action, and long-held hopes for radical change. Whether they called for the universal equality of all people as coworkers in society, or the return of Jews to their ancestral home in Palestine, these parties gave their members concrete ways to work for survival, even salvation.

**A** blending of Zionist and socialist goals was achieved by members of *Halutz* (Pioneer) groups. Although some two thousand young Zionists fled from rural areas to Vilna in the fall of 1939, several thousand others maintained their experimental farm settlements to prepare themselves for *aliyah* to Palestine. There they studied agriculture as well as Zionist ideas, matters quite distant from the world of the city ghettos in which most Jews lived. But by late 1941, the Germans ordered some of these *kibbutzim* closed, and financial support from the Jewish community was decreasing as well. In a short time, most Zionist youth were back in the ghettos, but they still were loyal to the ideals of Zionism and worked in various parties and youth movements to keep interest in Palestine alive.

The strongest underground political movement in the ghetto was the socialist Jewish workers' association, the *Bund*. From its headquarters in Warsaw, the Bund kept printing a daily newspaper by hand, even throughout the German siege of the city. Early in the German occupation, the Bund organized public kitchens, a Socialist Red Cross to care for the sick and those on forced labor, and a youth movement. The Bund also trained a party militia, like the militias it set up to fight pogroms in Russia earlier in the century, to defend the Jewish community as best it could.

The first task of the parties and youth organizations was survival. "Even in those days," a member of Dror wrote about the first months of the German occupation of Vilna, "one of the most important tasks was to procure bread for the hungry." Some parties received money from the Judenräte or the Self-Help association to carry on their welfare tasks, and while the first goal was to care for party members, all the movements reached out into the general population of the ghettos. Since parties were illegal, their work had to be carried on in secret, and members commonly forged papers, acted as couriers by posing as Poles, and risked their lives to keep party unity alive. Among the

Ḥalutz couriers was a group of young women whose bravery became legendary. "They are a theme," Ringelblum noted, "that calls for the pen of a great writer."

Early in 1941, the Bund office in Warsaw reported to its New York organization and described the party's goals:

*1. To strengthen the power of resistance and endurance of the Jewish masses in the face of unheard-of terrible persecutions without parallel in human history. . . .*

*2. To inform the Jewish populace about the resistance and struggle against the occupants beyond the borders of the Jewish ghettos both in Poland and in all occupied countries.*

*3. To implant the firm conviction that though the Jewish masses may be persecuted, the majority will nevertheless survive and live to see the conclusive defeat of the enemy.*

All groups shared that will to survive, and most believed that the Germans would be defeated in the war. While the Nazis spoke of destroying the Jews, the Bund saw its struggle as a universal, not particularly Jewish, one. In May 1940, the Bund's Central Committee issued this policy statement:

*Poland is our homeland, where we are entitled to equal citizenship rights, where our future lies. . . . Any other solutions offered, under present conditions, by Zionist or other Jewish groups, are wrong and utopian, as they always were. Together with the Polish working masses struggling underground, the Jewish people of Poland see no other means of survival, but the defeat of Hitlerism and the reconstruction of a free, independent, and Socialist Poland.*

Zionist groups were less committed to life in Europe, more to the future of Palestine as a Jewish homeland. On May 1, 1941, Dror proclaimed loyalty to Zionism and socialism:

*The struggle with the Hitlerite conqueror has temporarily separated us from Eretz Israel, but just as there is no power in the world that can separate us from the struggle for a socialist world, thus nothing can separate us from the land of our ultimate hope. The building of Eretz Israel is undeniably connected with the collapse of capitalism; a socialist Eretz*

*Israel will rise or fall with the success or failure of socialism.*
The previous May Day, a socialist holiday, was the very day when Jews in Lodz were enclosed in a ghetto. While Jewish socialist groups hoped that the "heroic Red Army" of Soviet Russia would save them and the world from Hitler, they were wrong. The best the Bundists could do that day was to pass out red-ribboned flowers and urge their fellow Jews to "hold on and hold out."

THE
UNDERGROUND
PRESS

The best way for parties to uphold the morale of their members and to promote the general struggle for survival was through the underground press. Publication was illegal, and the penalty for possession of a radio was death. But secret bulletins were printed and distributed by the hundreds, and some ghetto Jews managed to monitor foreign radio news broadcasts in secret. Nothing could be left for the Germans to find, so papers were passed around, then destroyed. Party members continually were urged to speak about news only with trusted friends and never to talk about party leaders or publication procedures.

Despite the Nazi censorship of news, then, the Jews were able to keep up with military and political developments in the war. Editorials in the underground press predicted the ultimate defeat of Hitler and encouraged readers to remain strong and hopeful.

*At times you think that things have come to their end, that you are no longer capable of doing anything. You are mistaken if you think so. Do not let apathy and despair overpower you, or even influence you. Harness yourself to hard, intensive work, work as hard as you can.*

In the summer of 1940, Dror published a 114-page mimeographed booklet called "Suffering and Heroism," which outlined the history of Jewish resistance to persecution since the Crusades. Nazism, it argued, like other anti-Semitic movements, would soon pass from history. Therefore, "we can conquer our own depression and not lose hope for a better future." The authors took pride in their tradition: "We are an old cultural people with a rich spiritual heritage from which we draw amply. We cannot and will not succumb, for we have survived similar hardships countless times in our three thousand-year-old history." The underground press intensified popular hostility toward the Judenräte and the police. The Bund advertised in its weekly paper. "Workers, hide and don't let yourselves be caught." Those unfortunate enough to "fall into the enemies' hands" were told that "the slogan of the working class in all occupied lands is *Work badly and slowly*." The Bund also decided to fight back against Nazi-sponsored Polish pogroms. In March 1940, a Warsaw Jewish militia armed itself with brass knuckles and iron pipes, weapons which successfully repelled their attackers without killing anyone as guns or knives might, and the anticipated German reprisals never came.

On some occasions, when hunger and misery grew intolerable, the parties carried out demonstrations and strikes with much popular support. In several cases, just the threat of a public strike won important demands from the Judenräte, though many times the Germans, using paid informers, were able to break up such activities while they were still in the planning stages. Quite early the Bund required a solemn oath

The front page of an underground Yiddish newspaper. The bottom caption reads: "War on Fascism."

of "loyalty unto death" for its members, a promise never to betray the organization. Each party suffered severe losses as its activists were discovered. In 1941, in Lublin, a Bundist who had been distributing anti-Nazi literature was caught by the Germans and publicly hanged.

In Warsaw, late Friday night, April 17, 1942, some fifty Jews were seized in their homes by the Gestapo and shot on the street. That night became known as "Bloody Friday." Most of those murdered were associated with the underground press, and the Gestapo warned that there would be more "executions" as long as the Jewish press continued to publish. The Bundist weekly argued in an editorial two weeks later that the struggle had to continue. Rather than "dishonor

Planting vegetables in the ghetto, an activity of TOPOROL, the society for the promotion of agriculture among Jews.

the peace of the martyrs," all Jews should resist the Nazis' brutal attempt to destroy them.

**The Rise of Socialism** Socialism developed from the early nineteenth century onward as several European thinkers began to consider the problem of the common laborer. It seemed only fair that the worker should share in the profits of his labor, indeed that the entire economic system should be organized so that property and production would be owned by the masses of people who worked rather than by a few bosses who were getting rich. As socialism grew, its goal of emancipating the worker was very much like the emancipation Jews were beginning to enjoy throughout Western Europe. While many socialists accepted old anti-Semitic theories about how Jews selfishly controlled world business, most believed that Jews should join the workers' struggle as equals.

Some Jews came to regard themselves more as socialists than Jews, but others strove to find a brand of socialism which would help solve the special difficulties faced by the Jewish people. Late in the nineteenth century, particularly in the Pale of Settlement, Jewish socialism played a major role in the revival of Hebrew and Yiddish, and in the growth of early Zionism. It is interesting to compare the socialist idea with the Jewish dictum, "The earth is the Lord's (Exodus 9:29; Deuteronomy 10:14; Psalms 24:1)."

**The Importance of Free Communication**   Hitler's use of propaganda and his attempts to stifle free speech were essential tactics in the Final Solution. The longer the truth could be hidden, the longer the Jews could be made to believe whatever Hitler wanted them to believe. For their part, Jews tried to keep lines of communication open both within occupied Europe and to the outside world.

Just as the Bill of Rights of the Constitution of the United States protects free speech and the free press, Jews throughout history have depended on truthful public communication as a safeguard for liberty and communal cooperation. The Torah, according to tradition, was received and transmitted in public; and rabbinic authorities often used public announcements during worship or public letters to reply to the legal questions of distant and often isolated Jewish communities. The first modern Jewish newspaper was published in 1675 in Amsterdam, only fifty-three years after the first modern English newspaper came into being. By the twentieth century there were hundreds of Hebrew and Yiddish papers throughout Europe. Many, of course, did not survive the Holocaust, but some six hundred are published currently outside Israel.

CHAPTER SEVENTEEN

# WHO SHALL LIVE, WHO SHALL DIE

**(Facing page) Deportees peer from a truck.**

Like a tornado the Nazi Special Duty Groups swept through the Jewish settlements in Eastern Europe in the summer of 1941. Virtually everywhere, the Germans found local non-Jews to help them. Many Lithuanians and Ukranians had for long years held superstitious anti-Semitic beliefs, and now they were able to turn these beliefs into action. Jews were captured on the streets and even in house-to-house searches and hauled away, supposedly for work. Massive pogroms saw thousands of Jews killed on the spot, even more carried off. Within hours or days, the SS machine-gunned the masses of captured Jews in some unpopulated area remote from town.

Jewish leaders and relatives and friends of those seized pleaded with and bribed German authorities to stop the pogroms and release captives who were still alive. Many Jews panicked hysterically, while others became paralyzed by fear and depression. Some even clung to hopes that their loved ones had not been killed but merely taken away for forced labor in some distant place, that surely they would return in the best of health at the war's end.

Wild mass violence slowed after a month. The Germans then began to organize more systematic and disciplined programs of murder. In Kovno, for instance, in August 1941, the Germans demanded from the Judenrat five hundred educated young men. These intellectuals, they said, were needed for work in the government archives and would therefore be spared from the heavy labor soon to be demanded from all Jews. The Judenrat prepared a list, and many young men

142

**Jews being forced to dig their own graves.**

volunteered their services for this seemingly desirable assignment. In all, 534 young educated Jews were taken away and never seen again. Similar tricks were used in other cities in a deliberate plan to destroy the most talented and influential members of the Jewish communities.

DISASTER AT KOVNO

Because the German army constantly was in need of supplies and equipment repairs, the military took over existing industries and put them to work for the war effort. Each Jewish worker in these factories and workshops was issued an identity card, or work permit. These permits became important symbols of security, for Jews expected that the Germans would keep alive any skilled laborer who might be able to aid in the continuing military campaign against Russia. This conviction led many Jews to register as workers with the Judenrat's labor office.

On September 15, 1941, the Germans sealed off the Kovno ghetto and stopped allowing workers to leave for outside labor. The next day, authorities delivered five thousands permits for skilled workers to the Judenrat, with orders for their distribution. Nearly thirty thousand Jews then lived in the ghetto, and some six thousand to seven thousand had already been murdered by SS Special Duty Groups. Several hours after the Judenrat officials received the cards, a German official at a factory called to make sure that "his" workers would receive what he described as their "life permits." Instantly, the Judenrat leaders understood that distribution of work cards really required deciding who would live and, because of Nazi plans, who would die.

The Judenrat officials called an emergency meeting. What should they do? Some suggested returning all the permits to the Germans with a statement that the Judenrat could not and would not distribute them. Others even advocated burning the cards. The whole Kovno Jewish community seemed doomed, so was it right to save one-sixth just to serve German plans? "If we must die, let us all die together." Meanwhile, news of the situation spread, and panic swept the ghetto. A mob of thousands of Jews — mostly workers — swarmed to the Judenrat, broke in, smashing doors and furniture, searching for the permits, shouting, "The cards belong to us." They seized the remaining cards, after Judenrat staff and Jewish policemen had already grabbed many for themselves.

All that night the Lithuanian police guarding the ghetto kept shooting, causing even greater terror and panic among the trapped Jews. In the morning, Germans and Lithuanians armed with machine guns assembled all the Jews in the small ghetto and began separating permit holders from the others. All at once, a Gestapo official drove up with a written message for the SS officer in charge of the selection process. Upon reading it, he ordered his men back to their barracks without any explanation.

On September 26, German police again surrounded the ghetto, on the grounds that Jews had shot a German policeman. One thousand people — mostly the old, the sick, and the widowed — were removed to an old fort and shot. The next week rumors were spread that a leprosy epidemic had struck the ghetto. A medical commission investigation found nothing. Just a few days later, Germans set fire to the ghetto hospital, and its patients and medical staff were burned alive.

The Kovno ghetto lived in unbearable tension and constant mourning for the dead. Rumors spread wildly, since people were willing to believe anything, good or bad. Everyone anticipated catastrophe. On October 28, the twenty-six thousand four hundred Jews of the

Kovno ghetto assembled by families, as ordered, in a large square. The SS had informed them that food rations were no longer available for Jews who could not perform heavy labor. By a flick of the German commandant's finger, large families and older people were directed into a group separate from the others. Nearly ten thousand people were kept overnight in an isolated small ghetto. The next morning they were marched out in columns and shot.

Those who survived were told that the "process" was now over, and to return to work. Drained of feeling, physically numb, they could not even weep. Fear alone thrived, and the words of Deuteronomy expressed daily reality:

> *And thy life shall hang in doubt before thee; and thou shalt fear night and day, and shalt have no assurance of thy life. In the morning thou shalt say: "Would it were evening!" and at evening thou shalt say: "Would it were morning!" for the fear of thy heart which thou shalt fear, and for the sight of thine eyes which thou shalt see.*

HALACHAH AND PERSECUTION

When the Judenrat of Kovno had been unable to decide whether or not to comply with the Germans' order to assemble on that fateful day in October, they asked Kovno's Chief Rabbi to issue a ruling on the basis of *Halachah*, Jewish law. Weakened by age, illness, and the terrible events of the recent past, Rabbi Abraham Dov Shapiro pored over rabbinic texts all night. Late the following morning, he ruled: If a community of Jews is threatened by persecution, and some may be saved in any way, then the leaders of the community must muster the courage and responsibility to rescue as many as possible. The Jews of Kovno therefore agreed to comply with the German order, despite its expected horrifying consequences.

For many centuries, Halachah had guided Jews in the Diaspora not only in ritual matters, but in all social, economic, political, and moral issues. Despite the rise of secularism in modern times, Halachah continued to retain full validity for observant Jews, and it provided guidance even for nonobservant Jews in difficult times which posed complex moral issues affecting the whole Jewish community. No Jewish community had ever before faced a threat of annihilation comparable to the one which now terrorized the Jews of Kovno and other European cities. In their history the Jews had been subject to slaughter, enslavement, kidnapping, and dire economic and religious discrimination. When rabbis attempted to find the proper response to such situations, they usually referred to a Talmudic case in which a third-century sage, Joshua ben Levi, advised his community to hand over a political fugitive to the Romans rather than risk being destroyed for not cooperating. Later interpretations of this case varied. Maimonides, for example, did not encourage cooperation with the authorities:

> . . . If heathens said to Israelites, "Surrender one of your number to us, that we may put him to death, otherwise, we will put all of you to death," they should all suffer death rather than surrender a single Israelite to them. But if they specified an individual, saying "Surrender that particular person to us, or else we will put all of you to death," they may give him up, provided that he was guilty of a capital crime. . . . If the individual specified has not incurred capital punishment, they should all suffer death rather than surrender a single Israelite to them.

In many ghettos the rabbis wrestled with Maimonides' ruling. Chief Rabbi Shapiro of Kovno was one of the few who disagreed with Maimonides. He concluded that some Jews must be surrendered if others could thereby be saved.

---

**W**hat happened in Kovno would take place again and again—in Vilna, Lodz, Lublin, and dozens of other cities and towns. In each location, the Germans and the Jews would act under slightly different circumstances, but the outcomes would vary only in detail. In Vilna, ten thousand persons, nearly half the Jewish community, were left unprotected by work permits. In Lodz, twenty thousand were ordered "exported," and in Lublin thirty thousand were taken—leaving only four thousand.

FURTHER "PROCESSES"

The "process" always involved dividing the Jews into categories. Children under twelve and adults over sixty-five were commonly designated as "unfit," and lists of "harmful" and "unproductive" Jews were demanded by the Germans as well. Those scheduled for deportation often tried desperate schemes to escape their fate— bribery or forgery to acquire work permits, secret hideouts, scrambling for "Vitamin P," even fasting and reciting psalms. "We are like animals surrounded by the hunter," a young man wrote in his dairy,

A child's drawing
shows a German
soldier shooting
at a train of
deportees.

describing his hideout.

> *I feel the enemy under the boards I stand on. . . . They pound, tear, break. . . . Suddenly, somewhere upstairs, a baby starts crying. . . . We are lost. A desperate attempt to shove sugar into the baby's mouth doesn't help. They stop its mouth with pillows. Its mother weeps. In wild terror people demand that the baby be strangled. The baby's wails grow louder; the Lithuanians pound more heavily against the walls.*

---

**ISSUES AND VALUES**

**Jewish Law—Halachah**   The Bible is only the beginning of Jewish law. Besides this "Written" form the law took an "Oral" form which was later recorded in writing. Thus, to explain the Bible, the rabbis developed a technique called *midrash*, מִדְרָשׁ , or "searching." Midrash applies biblical principles to new and changing situations. Similarly, the Palestinian rabbis developed a Mishnah and Talmud and the Babylonian rabbis developed a Talmud which commented on the Palestinian Mishnah, amplifying and extending its legal discussion.

In addition, *minhag*, מִנְהָג , or local custom, has always

148

been a source of oral tradition, as have the *takkanot*, תַּקָּנוֹת , the "ordinances" of particular rabbis and the *responsa*, תְּשׁוּבוֹת , the legal letters of "answering" published by central rabbinical authorities.

Since the ninth century, various scholars have attempted to codify halachah, producing such works as the *Mishneh Torah* of Maimonides and the *Shulḥan Aruch* of Joseph Caro. Modern Jews differ in their approaches to the halachah of past generations, but all agree that it is an important source of practical and spiritual guidance. The word *halachah*, הֲלָכָה , itself comes from the Hebrew verb meaning "to walk," and indicates the rabbinic idea that the law was the proper path to follow.

**"Fitness"** While the ultimate goal of the Final Solution was the destruction of all Jews, Hitler consistently singled out certain kinds of individuals for early annihilation on the grounds that they were particularly "unfit." The very young and very old, as well as those suffering from mental or physical illnesses, were regarded by the Nazis as persons of "little value." Against this immoral stance, Jewish tradition affirms the worth of all human beings, since each is created in the image of God. From the first day of life a child is legal heir to his parents' estate in the eyes of halachah (Niddah 5:3), and even a dying person's words have legal force in business or inheritance matters (Baba Batra 9:6–7, Ketubot 48a, 103a). The rabbis recognized that newborn infants die of natural causes more often than children who are older, but they rightly say that anyone who kills a child even one day old is to be regarded as a murderer (Niddah 5:3).

# CHAPTER EIGHTEEN

# "FOR YOUR FREEDOM AND OURS"

(Facing page) Karl Schwesig, a non-Jew interred in Gurs, a concentration camp in France, drew these stamps on the blank borders of a sheet of postage stamps. The words—"Liberty," "Equality," and "Fraternity"—were the motto of the French Revolution. The stamps tell ironically what Schwesig believed had become of these noble ideas.

The great wave of killings and deportations of Eastern European Jews led the youth of the Jewish political movements to organize armed resistance to the Germans. So many families had been destroyed that almost no younger children or aging parents in need of care remained. Young people were now free from family responsibilities and had no one but themselves to protect from German reprisals. Most of all, the resistance movement was spurred on by the knowledge of the death camps and the sense of death's inevitability. There was no further reason to cooperate with the Nazis: "One way or another lies death."

Despair over Jewish powerlessness and a burning desire to take revenge against the Germans had converted many young political leaders to a new outlook. Their educational and cultural programs in the ghetto had been based on hopes for eventual improvements in Jewish life, but by now they realized that the Germans meant to destroy all Jews. Precious time, they felt, had been "wasted"—Jewish history and the arts were less important than learning about weapons and defense strategies.

These young people in the Zionist and socialist movements rejected traditional Judaism's passivity in the face of martyrdom. For centuries, Jews in the Diaspora had accepted powerlessness as a decree from God. Now young resistance leaders could not believe that they should be, as the Psalms say, "sheep for the slaughter." If they had to die, it would be as "men of honor."

150

As early as the turn of the century, the new socialist and Zionist movements had armed themselves in self-defense units to ward off pogroms. In the Nazi ghettos, however, everyone realized that the SS were far more powerful and organized a war machine than any horde of drunken peasants or company of Cossack horsemen. Besides, acts of resistance early in the war would certainly have cost many lives in Germany reprisal attacks. By 1943, however, the young people who survived understood that no option but death existed. Resistance was hardly likely to save the remaining Jews in the ghetto, but by defying the Germans with whatever armed strength they could muster, they would defend the honor of the Jews.

Resistance was therefore not so much self-defense as it was an act of desperation. As the first-century defenders of Masada had committeed mass suicide rather than surrender to the Roman legions, members of the resistance chose to die in their own way, not by the German plan. The modern Hebrew poet Yitzhak Lamdan had written about Masada in words cherished by the Zionist movement: "We have one treasure left—the daring after despair." One might strive for glory now, but realistically. "We are going on the road to death, remember that," one activist said. "Whoever desires still to live should not search for life here among us. We are at the end."

One feeling members of all resistance groups shared was a passionate hatred for the Germans. One woman in a Dror kibbutz in Bialystok wrote to comrades in Palestine about underground production of grenades: "We'll kill our slaughterers; they will have to fall together with us." She charged her friends: "We call you to vengeance, revenge without remorse or mercy. . . . Vengeance! This is our challenge to you, who have not suffered in Hitler's hell. This you are duty-bound to fulfill. Our scattered bones will not rest in peace, the scattered ashes of the crematoria will not lie still, until you have avenged us."

---

ORGANIZING THE STRUGGLE

The first resistance organization was set up in Vilna by about 150 young Zionists who met on January 1, 1942. This United Partisans Organization came to represent the major Zionist, Socialist, and Communist youth movements, all of whom were now dedicated to defending Jewish dignity and avenging the murder of Jews. Later in 1942, the Jewish Combat Organization was formed in Warsaw, again guided by the existing political parties. Young people understood that any mistake they might make would easily prove disastrous for the Jewish community. Although the resistance groups would be daring, they would try not to be reckless. Other Jewish leaders had to be consulted, and all possible help had to be sought. One resistance leader warned, "Don't think, comrades, that just because you have two broken revolvers, you can be hoity-toity and take no account of anyone else."

One important concern was maintaining contact with the outside world—the underground Polish Home Army, the Polish government-in-exile, and Jewish parties in Palestine and the United States. Even in places not under Nazi rule, heroic resistance acts were possible. On May 12, 1943, Arthur Zygelboym, a forty-eight-year-old Bundist who had fled Warsaw four years earlier, took his life in London. His farewell letter read:

S. M. (Arthur) Zygelboym, a leader of the Jewish Labor Bund. He committed suicide on May 11, 1943, in London, in protest against the indifference of the world to the destruction of Polish Jewry.

> *I cannot be silent. I cannot live while the remnants of the Jewish population of Poland, of whom I am a representative, are perishing. My friends in the Warsaw ghetto died with weapons in their hands in the last heroic battle. It was not my destiny to die together with them but I belong to them and in their mass graves.*
>
> *By my death I wish to make my final protest against the passivity with which the world is looking on and permitting the extermination of the Jewish people.*

Throughout Europe, hundreds of non-Jews were also fighting underground against the Nazis. Patriots of German-occupied lands were struggling to aid the Allied armies, to boost morale and keep information about the war flowing. But the Jewish resistance effort was the most desperate one. One Zionist leader said, "We are not going to die in slow torment, but fighting. We will declare war on Germany—the most hopeless declaration of war that has even been made." Another confirmed: "We are organizing a defense of the ghetto, not because we think it can be defended, but to let the world see the hopelessness of our battle—as a demonstration and a reproach."

---

**I**n each ghetto, practical questions of how to acquire weapons, where to fight, and when to fight became matters of life and death. Decisions had to be made in consultation with the Judenräte, alternative communal leadership, and the political underground. As

STRATEGIES

153

long as those leaders believed that the ghetto might survive, because the Soviet army was approaching or because the Jews were important to the German war economy, policies of active resistance were not supported. The underground parties restricted their operations to protecting their people until the moment of liberation. On June 6, 1944, news of the Allied invasion of Normandy stirred the ghettos to joy, and Jews began to believe that they were likely to survive. Soon, however, the Germans began to speed up the deportations, and most attempts at resistance proved futile.

Ghetto leaders who were pessimistic about the war's developments gave resistance groups moral and financial support, but rarely did they endorse resistance plans. Some Jewish resisters joined with Soviet partisans in guerrilla army units detached from the ghettos, while others—particularly Zionist youth—favored making last stands inside ghetto walls. For the most part, ghetto Jews regarded these young people who plotted armed resistance as irresponsible hotheads who would bring disaster upon the whole ghetto. In a small town near Vilna, observant Jews even gathered in a synagogue to excommunicate ten young people who intended to join partisans fighting in the woods.

Everywhere, the Germans employed lies, surprise, and cunning to liquidate the ghettos. At night or at dawn, they would suddenly encircle a Jewish area to prevent resistance combat groups from having the opportunity to mobilize. Sometimes, Jews would spontaneously resist out of a desire for last revenge. In some small towns, those the Nazis caught and killed were actually outnumbered by those who were able to flee to the forest or commit suicide rather than be captured. On September 23, 1942, two young men agitated the Tuczyn ghetto population of some two thousands Jews not to obey German orders to assemble. "Don't go voluntarily!" "Don't you know that the mass pits are dug already?" Then someone shouted: "Set fire!" Everyone began to bring kerosene, in pitchers, kettles, jugs, and cups, to their workshops and to their homes. That evening they destroyed their possessions so the Germans would not be able to confiscate them. Soon the whole ghetto was aflame. The Germans and Ukranians surrounding the ghetto were caught unawares and began shooting into the flames. In that confusion, most of the Jews managed to break through the ghetto enclosures and flee from the burning ghetto into the woods.

**The Issue of Self-Defense**   Jewish thinkers have often discussed the rights of self-defense. If life is threatened and no alternative is available, the person threatened is entitled even to kill in self-defense (Exodus 22:1–2). Beginning in the time of the Maccabean Revolt, this principle was extended to allow for defensive warfare, if necessary, even on Shabbat.

Following the examples of many medieval Jewish communities the Jews of East Europe resisted as best they could the pogroms of the late nineteenth and early twentieth centuries. The socialist and Zionist movements were prominent in these resistance efforts, as were yeshivah students and ordinary laborers. Sometimes, calling upon a kind of romantic flair, the ancient symbol of the shofar called Jewish fighters into battle.

**A Tradition of Protest**   The patriarch Abraham, the first Jew, began the history of protest in Judaism when he demanded that God not kill the innocent minority of people during the destruction of Sodom and Gomorrah. "Will You indeed sweep away the righteous with the wicked?" he asked. "Shall not the Judge of all the earth do justly?" (Genesis 18:23, 25) This example of protest, even against God, was followed by the prophets of ancient Israel who decried injustice and yet pleaded with the Lord to be merciful. Rabbinic literature makes clear the rights of individuals to protest, for example against unfair seizure of property (Sukkot 29b, Baba Batra 38b–39a). Women are also allowed to dispute conditions of marriage when it is arranged by their parents (Ketubot 68b). And legend has it that the ancient rabbi Ḥoni successfully demanded that God send rain in a time of drought. Ḥoni drew a circle on the ground, stepped inside of it, and announced to heaven that he would not move until it rained (Taanit 3:8). More recently, the Hasidic rabbi Levi Yitzhak used the occasion of Yom Kippur to protest his people's case against God.

# THE WARSAW GHETTO

By the last week of 1941, horrifying news of mass deportations and annihilation of Jews had reached the Warsaw ghetto. Couriers and escapees had arrived from Vilna, Lodz, Bialystok, and even from the Chełmno death camp to give their agonizing reports. But the Bundist underground newspaper carried these stories on the third or fourth page, giving far more prominence to news about military developments. Perhaps the editors disbelieved the accounts, or at least they felt that Warsaw would not be directly affected.

The Warsaw underground movement was not sure how to respond. On the one hand, both accurate reports and exaggerated rumors brought panic to the ghetto. Such hysteria undermined morale, and besides, the stories were indeed difficult to believe. On the other hand, the Jews of Warsaw had to be warned and prepared in case there would be a need for self-defense. Therefore, the Bundist paper felt obligated in February 1942 to print these details, now on the second page, of the gas-van killing procedure at Chełmno: "The 'execution' lasts fifteen minutes, accompanied by the roar of the motor which is set in operation to drown out the screams and groans of the tortured, defenseless victims." By early April, another Warsaw underground paper carried a lead article about mass deportations from Lublin: "The Jewish Population Under the Sign of Physical Annihilation."

156

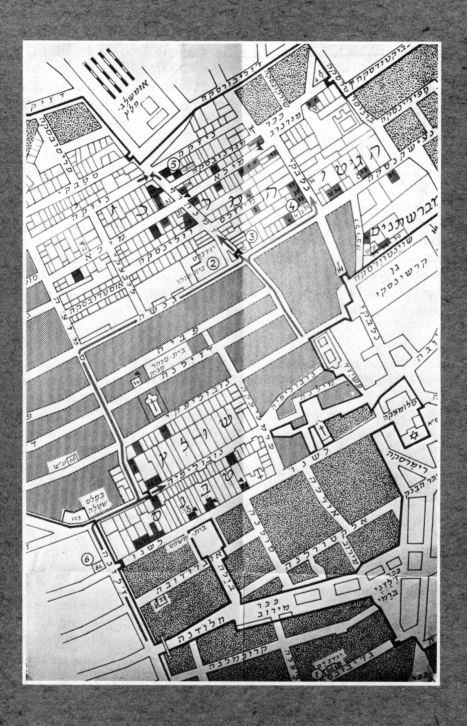

**T**hroughout the spring of 1942, the ghetto lived on the edge of disaster. Every Warsaw Jew must have heard something about mass deportations, from the illegal press or radio, or elsewhere. Many had met Jews who had escaped from the death camps and listened in shock to their tales of horror. Against this backdrop, a series of unusual events brought the ghetto to near-panic. On April 29, the ghetto commissar requested from the Judenrat population statistics by streets and buildings, and on the same day another German official asked for ten maps of the ghetto. On May 4, lists of all workers, including community officials, were demanded, and rumors of impending mass deportations of "unproductive" Jews began to sweep the ghetto. In the beginning of July, 110 imprisoned Jews were shot, and on July 18 forty freight cars arrived at a railroad siding, evidence to nearly everyone of impending doom. Nevertheless, on July 20 a German official assured the head of the Judenrat, Adam Czerniaków, that rumors about deportations were "rubbish" and "nonsense."

The next morning, some forty Judenrat officials and staff were taken hostage. Czerniaków was left free but his wife was seized. One day later, the ghetto was surrounded, and the special police issued typed orders to the Jews of Warsaw. All of them, regardless of age or sex, were to be "resettled" in the East, except for those employed by German enterprises, Judenrat staff, Jewish police, and Jewish hospital personnel and their families. The deportation was to start within one hour.

The instructions specified that the Judenrat would be responsible for delivering six thousand Jews daily to the place of assembly. Any Jew who left the ghetto without authorization or acted to evade or interfere with resettlement procedures would be shot. If the Judenrat did not comply one hundred percent with its instructions, "an appropriate number of hostages . . . will be shot in each instance." Czerniaków tried to convince the German officials to change the orders if only slightly, particularly to exempt orphans. He won a few minor reprieves for municipal workers, vocational students, and husbands of working women. But the children would not be saved, and Czerniaków was informed that if plans were resisted, his wife would be the first hostage to be shot. Unable to carry on, he took a cyanide tablet he had kept ready, leaving suicide notes to his wife and colleagues: "I am powerless. My heart trembles in sorrow and compassion. I can no longer bear all this. My act will prove to everyone what is the right thing to do." One of his Jewish critics later eulogized him: "He perpetuated his name by his death more than by his life."

Jews rounded up and arrested by German troops in the Warsaw Ghetto.

Once the deportations began, the Jewish leaders in Warsaw struggled with the same questions of strategy that had plagued other communities. The majority opposed resistance, believing it would bring on German reprisals which would wipe out the entire community. The youth movements advocated active resistance, while the Bund urged nonviolent passive disobedience to German orders and to the Jewish police. No one plan pleased all, and the rounding up of six thousand Jews became a daily routine.

The Germans used fear cleverly and ruthlessly. The Jewish police performed their hated functions diligently because they themselves were constantly subjected to death threats. One policeman, trying to grab a child from its father, exclaimed: "What makes you think I'm human? Maybe I'm a wild beast. I have a wife and three children. If I don't deliver my five heads by five P.M., they'll take my children. Don't you see, I'm fighting for the life of my own kids?"

The Germans took advantage of the people's hunger. They

announced that persons who reported voluntarily for resettlement would receive free rations of bread and marmalade, and thousands of Jews came forward. The situation was so hopeless that parents who could not see beyond tomorrow regarded resettlement as a way of keeping their family together. Deep in their hearts, most could not believe that they were being deported to their deaths, and resistance seemed to be little more than suicide. Indeed, German cruelty had increased until now "the Jews came to fear the Germans more than death."

---

THE CAULDRON    On September 5, the Germans announced that all Jews in the Warsaw ghetto, without exception, were to assemble the following morning for registration, with food for two days and drinking utensils. Whoever did not comply would be shot. The whole day passed with a sense that death had come, wrote a scholar who was now a factory worker. No possibility existed for escape from "the clutches of the wild beast. . . . We are only prolonging our death agony."

The Germans called the procedure an *Einkesselung* ("encirclement"), but the Jews described it in Yiddish as a *kesl* ("cauldron"). For one week police surrounded the Jews, and nearly ten thousand were deported each day. And, in addition to deportation, there was murder. That week ended on Rosh Hashanah, and by that holy day 2,648 Jews had been shot to death.

The ghetto was cut into four tiny, isolated sections. The surviving Jews lived at their factories or in hiding. Jewish home life and the Jewish family had been destroyed. Of the more than three hundred fifty thousand Jews in the Warsaw ghetto on July 22, 1942, only forty-five thousand or so remained. The streets were strewn with dead Jewish bodies. On Yom Kippur the Germans made one last roundup of two thousand persons, including some six hundred Jewish policemen.

From the ashes of the Warsaw ghetto, a new underground paper, *On Guard*, appeared on September 20. Its lead article, "The Annihilation of Warsaw Jews," urged its readers:

> *Today every Jew should know the fate of those resettled. The same fate awaits the remaining few left in Warsaw. The conclusion then is: Don't let yourself be caught! Hide, don't let yourself be taken away, run away, don't be fooled by*

*registrations, selections, numbers, and roll calls! Jews, help one another! Take care of the children! Help the illegals! The dishonorable traitors and helpers — the Jewish police — should be boycotted! Don't believe them, beware of them. Stand up against them!*

*We are all soldiers on a terrible front!*

*We must survive so that we can demand a reckoning for the tortured brothers and sisters, children and parents who were killed by the murderer's hand on the battlefield for freedom and humanity!*

The report came too late for the three hundred thousand Warsaw Jews already deported. But it heralded the resistance to come.

---

**The Ransoming of Captives**   Holding hostages for ransom has been a common tactic of anti-Semitic persecutors throughout Jewish history, particularly during the Crusades and later during pogroms in Eastern Europe. The Talmud says that ransoming such captives is a paramount religious responsibility (Baba Batra 2a–b), and Maimonides adds that this duty takes precedence even over charitable aid to the poor. Naturally, there is always the risk that the ransom will not succeed in freeing the captives, as was so often the case under the Nazis. Recently, the Israeli government has acted with force to try to end skyjacking and other kidnap attempts, on the theory that terrorism should never be condoned and ransoming the captives often leads to the taking of more captives.

**The Days of Awe**   The first ten days of the first month in the Jewish calendar, Tishri, is the period set aside for Jews to seek atonement from God for sins committed against Him in the past year. Prayers and fasting, together with the special worship on Rosh Hashanah and Yom Kippur, give time for personal introspection and seeking forgiveness for errors. According to the rabbis, God seals the fate of all Jews during this time, determining who shall live and who shall die in the year to follow. Tragically, persecutors of the Jewish people, like the Nazis, have often chosen precisely this time for their most evil actions.

# CHAPTER TWENTY

# WARSAW: THE LAST RESISTANCE

(Facing page) Mordecai Anielewicz, Commandant of the Jewish Combat Organization, which planned and carried out the Warsaw Ghetto uprising.

Organized Jewish resistance made its most vigorous and sustained stand against the Nazis in Warsaw. After the "cauldron" period in September 1942, leadership passed from the Judenrat and the political parties into the hands of the political and military underground—The Jewish Coordinating Committee and the Jewish Combat Organization. Warsaw was different from Bialystok and Kovno, where the Judenräte retained the confidence of the ghettos until the end. It was also unlike Lublin and Cracow, where the deportations and the collapse of the Judenräte left the Jewish communities without any leadership in their period of desperation. In Warsaw, the underground ably substituted for the fallen Judenrat, giving the surviving fifty thousand Jews information, guidance, some measure of hope, and a burning desire for revenge.

Thousands of Jews now lived underground illegally, in hideouts devised cleverly to conceal dozens or even hundreds of people for months on end. Water and food supplies were stored, entrances and passageways were concealed—a whole city thrived in secret. Knowing that large numbers of Jews had eluded them, the Germans told new lies to try to entice those in hiding to come forward. In late November 1942, the Germans offered amnesty, food, and employment to Jews willing to take advantage of the "new" situation.

To these falsehoods the Jewish Combat Organization responded vigorously. The mimeograph machine and the gun became the tools of leadership. German tricks were exposed by Jewish Combat

**Jews captured during the Warsaw Ghetto uprising.**

Organization leaflets, and Jewish traitors and Gestapo agents faced execution by the underground's weapons. Since the chief German strategy was to lie, the new Jewish stand was to "look the truth straight in the face." The survivors in the Warsaw ghetto were reminded constantly of the awful truth that the Germans aimed to destroy every one of them. The ghetto prepared to defend itself by force, if possible; otherwise, by hiding.

THE FIRST TEST

On January 18, 1943, German troops surrounded the ghetto, taking the Jewish leadership forces completely by surprise. Five units of the Jewish Combat Organization immediately counterattacked, even though the units were cut off from one another and unable to communicate. The Jewish fighters killed or wounded about fifty Germans, and the attempt to deport Jews was halted with only a small number having been seized. The Jewish Combat Organization had suffered extensive losses, but their bold resistance electrified the ghetto. There was proof that the Germans could be repelled, and their was hope for even greater success.

Resistance gained new supporters. Bakers volunteered bread for the fighters, and leatherworkers made them holsters. Even smugglers and black marketeers offered, out of their supplies, food and drink. Most of all, the Jewish Combat Organization needed money. This they raised by collecting "taxes" from whatever wealth remained in the ghetto, and by confiscating funds from the Judenrat treasury and the ghetto bank. Finally, the Jewish Combat Organization took measures to rid the community of traitors. In February 1943 alone, five Jewish Gestapo agents were shot to death, and a leaflet listing the crimes of each was published to warn others against working for the Germans.

After the losses in January, the Jewish Combat Organization was reorganized into twenty-two units, each consisting of at least eight men and no more than two women. New fighters were accepted only after careful examination. While there were many volunteers, weapons were extremely scarce. Morale among the members was high because each felt a sense of purpose and meaning in the work that had to be done, and in the responsibility for guarding each others' lives.

---

**A**fter the battle of January 18, the Jewish leaders in Warsaw were convinced that the Germans were preparing for the final liquidation of Polish Jewry. On January 21, the Jewish Coordinating Committee sent this secret radio message via the Polish government-in-exile to Jewish leaders in New York:   APPEALS

> We notify you of the greatest crime of all times, about the murder of millions of Jews in Poland. Poised at the brink of the annihilation of the still surviving Jews, we ask you:
> 1. Revenge against the Germans .
> 2. Force the Hitlerites to halt the murders
> 3. Fight for our lives and our honor
> 4. Contact the neutral countries
> 5. Rescue ten thousand children through exchange

> 6. *Five hundred thousand dollars for purposes of aid*
>
> *Brothers — the remaining Jews in Poland live with the awareness that in the most terrible days of our history you did not come to our aid. Respond, at least in the last days of our life.*

On February 7, underground Bund leaders radioed another urgent message: ". . . We suffer terribly. The surviving two hundred thousand await annihilation. Only you can save us. The responsibility with regard to history will rest on you."

Meanwhile, the Germans continued trying to deceive the Jews and lure them out of hiding. To make the propaganda more believable, the SS remained behind the scenes while German employers appealed to their workers to register for "resettlement," promising them "a life rich in magnificent amusements." But the Jewish Combat Organization retaliated by burning down factories and attacking by surprise to free Jewish prisoners. Increasingly, resistance fighters were seen by the ghetto Jews as their defenders. Still, by the spring of 1943, the need for outside aid was clearly urgent. Early in April, both the Jewish Coordinating Committee and the Bund sent radio appeals for help to London, Geneva, New York, and Jerusalem, crying, "Storm heaven and earth!"

---

THE FINAL
BATTLE

At 2:00 A.M. on Monday, April 19, 1943, armed German, Latvian, and Ukranian patrols began to encircle the Warsaw ghetto. Within a half-hour, the Jewish Combat Organization received news of this development, and by daylight its fighters were mobilized. At 6:00 A.M. two thousand SS troops entered the ghetto with tanks, rapid-fire guns, and three trailers of ammunition. The Jewish Combat Organization units attacked with explosive devices and guns. By 5:00 P.M. the Germans, surprised and shocked by the Jewish resistance, withdrew from the ghetto, having lost some two hundred dead and wounded.

"We were happy and laughing," said one Jewish fighter. "When we threw our grenades and saw German blood on the streets of Warsaw, which had been flooded with so much Jewish blood and tears, a great joy possessed us." Everyone knew that the Germans would return and ultimately would defeat the Jewish Combat Organization, but now Jews in the ghetto embraced and kissed each other. That April

**Mordecai Anielewicz among the fighting Jews, a drawing by a Jewish child (M. Engelman) of Poland made after the liberation.**

19 marked the celebration of the first Passover seder. Throughout the ghetto, the reading of the Haggadah was punctuated by gunfire and shell bursts.

Early the next morning, the Germans demanded that the Jews lay down their arms by ten o'clock. But SS troops entering the ghetto were met by grenades, mines, and gunfire. The Germans retaliated with tanks, field artillery, and heavy machine guns, and they warned that unless the Jews surrendered, the entire area would be bombed. But no Jews laid down their arms. The Germans began setting fire to ghetto buildings, and as pillars of smoke began to rise everywhere, they cut off the supplies of electricity, gas, and water from the ghetto streets. Yet the resistance troops fought on. For days the ghetto seethed in flames, but late in the first week of the struggle the Jewish Combat Organization proclaimed to all Poles:

> *Let it be known that every threshold in the ghetto has been and will continue to be a fortress, that we may all perish in this struggle, but we will not surrender; that, like you, we breathe with desire for revenge for all the crimes of our common foe.*

From then on the Jewish fighters could muster only isolated guerrilla attacks on the much stronger German forces. Time and space were running out. Food and water were nowhere to be found. All around, one resister wrote, was "the roar of the fire, the noise of falling walls. Outside the ghetto it was spring, but here a holocaust reigned."

On May 8, the Germans surrounded the hideout of the Jewish Combat Organization's headquarters. The civilians in the bunker surrendered, but over one hundred Jewish fighters held firm, preparing for their last battle. Instead, the Germans stuffed up all the entrances and sent gas into the bunker. One resister called out, "Let's not fall into their hands alive!" They began to kill themselves and each other in a scene reminiscent of the fall of Masada. Two days later, about seventy-five Jewish Combat Organization survivors from other parts of the ghetto made their way through the slime of Warsaw's sewers to escape, with the help of comrades on the "Aryan" side. The Warsaw ghetto had become one huge cemetery.

Resistance could not stop the liquidation of Polish Jewry. The destruction had proceeded too rapidly. The police, the camps, and the anti-Semitic Poles—all had seized the moment eagerly. The Jewish communities had disappeared. There were no more synagogues, no Jewish schools, no Jewish life to sustain. Blood-soaked debris of Yiddish and Hebrew books were all that remained of the thousand-year-old civilization of Jews in Poland.

---

ISSUES AND VALUES

**The Use of Capital Punishment** The Bible prescribes capital punishment in the forms of stoning, burning, or hanging for particularly serious crimes. The ancient rabbis, however, were careful to interpret these laws narrowly so that the death penalty would not be used unwisely. In fact, power to execute criminals had already passed to the Roman Imperial authorities, as can be seen from the story of Jesus' trial in the New Testament. So the deliberations of the rabbis on the question of capital punishment were theoretical, but if they had been applied in practice, virtually no one would ever have been put to death (Makkot 1:10).

In the difficult period of persecutions in Spain during the Middle Ages, Jewish communities sometimes asked civil authorities to put informers to death, but then and later excommunication—expelling an individual totally from the Jewish community—was a far more common punishment.

The modern State of Israel prescribes the death penalty only for murder and military treason in time of war, though this penalty has never been inflicted. Adolf Eichmann was put to death in 1962 in

Israel for the crime of genocide.

**Revenge**    Blood vengeance was the common response to murder in ancient times (Numbers 35) and the Bible makes it clear that under certain circumstances Jews were permitted to seek revenge (Exodus 21:12–14; Numbers 31:1–2; Psalms 149:7). In biblical terms, even God seeks revenge (Leviticus 26:25; Deuteronomy 32:43). At the same time, the Bible and later Jewish literature praises forgiveness (Leviticus 19:18). The Talmud compares two people to a pair of hands—if the left hand slips while slicing meat and cuts the right hand, should the right hand cut back?

In theory and in practice, the ancient pattern of blood-avenging gave way to systems of courts, so only in rare circumstances does halachah permit taking the law into one's own hands. The Holocaust was one of those rare circumstances—Jews had no choice.

# CHAPTER TWENTY-ONE

# THE JEWISH RESPONSE TO CRISIS

**T**he Final Solution was a new phenomenon in human history. Perhaps that is why most European Jews were unable to foresee the terrible consequences World War II held for them. The long Jewish past of persecution provided little guidance for strategies to combat Hitler. Early on, the Jews believed that the anti-Semitic policies of Nazi Germany were but another familiar episode in two thousand years of trials. Such explanations failed in the ultimate encounter with the Final Solution.

The responses of the Jewish community were based not only on their understanding of the present in the light of history, but also on Jewish tradition and its concepts of Jewish national identity. Despite all the disasters of Jewish history, Jews have been committed optimists because of Judaism's teachings. All creation, Genesis declares, is good. Whatever God does, the rabbis would say in times of distress, is for the best.

The tradition teaches that the whole world depends on justice, that good is rewarded and evil punished. All of life has order and meaning, even though people at times may not be able to understand their existence. This optimistic view of a rational, moral world was accepted even by Jews who in modern, secular times could not agree that God is the source of human goodness.

Preservation of life is one of the most important values in Judaism, and this religious principle motivated both individual and organized community activism for Jewish survival. The tradition

(Illustrations on this page, 173 and 175) The diary of Liesel Felsenthal shows life, hour-by-hour, in the concentration camp of Gurs, France. Each page was less than two inches square. Liesel was around 15 when she drew this diary; she died while being transported to Auschwitz.

171

teaches that life is sacred and must be safeguarded in whatever way possible. Thus though Jews prayed to God for mercy and help in times of distress, they did not passively wait for deliverance. They made every effort to seek protection from one power against the assault of another, to flee temporarily or emigrate permanently, to ransom hostages, and even to defend themselves militarily—all at great peril.

Since the destruction of the Second Temple in Jerusalem by the Romans in 70 C.E., the Jews had to live with the fact of their powerlessness. The rabbis in the Talmud and other religious teachings addressed this problem, and through them Judaism offered attitudes and values which gave meaning to Jewish survival. "Belong always to the persecuted rather than to the persecutors," the Talmud taught. "God loves the persecuted and hates the persecutors." Cautioning against rash rebellion, the rabbis advised their people to endure suffering but maintain hope, to make virtues of self-discipline, good judgment, and all possible nonviolent means of avoiding discrimination and combatting persecution.

THE HISTORY OF THE FINAL SOLUTION

The European Jews experienced three progressive stages of decline after the National Socialists came to power. The beginning stage lasted through the first six years of the German dictatorship until the "Night of Shattered Glass" in 1938. During this period Jews saw the benefits of their Emancipation fade. The second stage was symbolized by the ghetto and the yellow star, and Jews saw themselves returning to the darkest days of the Middle Ages, when they were the most scorned and least powerful of the people. The third stage, annihilation, began with the mass killings by the Special Duty Groups in 1941 and continued until the end of the war with the operation of the death camps. This period was without precedent or rational explanation.

With these perceptions of their situation, the Jewish leaders and masses evaluated the Final Solution and tried to find strategies for self-defense. Tactics had to be weighed in terms of costs and benefits, then compared with alternative measures. Policy was always two-pronged: directed internally to strengthen the community and bolster its morale; directed outwardly, in dealings with the oppressor, to lessen hardships and combat persecutions.

Jewish communal leaders faced enormous difficulties trying to understand and respond to the crises of these years. Each act they

von 13-14ᵘ Brot-
holen

von 14-15ⁿ am
Tieretschalter

von 15-16ᵘ Zucker-
holen

von 16ⁿ-17ⁿ wird die Wäsche
aufgehängt

von 17ⁿ-18ʰ Wasser-
holen

von 18ⁿ-19ʰ das Essen
kommt -
HURRA!

committed or failed to commit was judged good or evil by their contemporaries. Now their opportunities, wisdom and intentions as well as their successes and failures, remain to be judged in the light of history.

---

DISEMANCIPATION, THE LOSS OF EQUALITY

**T**he Jewish community and its leaders were not surprised that the National Socialist dictatorship promoted anti-Jewish propaganda and legislation in the first stage of its rule. But nearly all Jews were certain Hitler could not retain power for long. The general strategy was for the Jews to resist yielding their rights, while at the same time trying to negotiate, bargain, and petition favor from the government.

Trying to hold on and hold out, the community rallied together. During this stage and the ones to follow, Jewish unity made possible the tasks of building morale and organizing self-help. But the community soon realized that although it could achieve these internal goals, the external situation was not encouraging. There were few friends or allies to help reverse trends of legal and economic decline, and the Nuremberg Laws and the "Night of Shattered Glass" proved that the Jews would not easily escape from their oppression.

---

GHETTOIZATION

**T**he second stage in the Jewish situation came with the German invasion of Poland in September 1939. Now it appeared that Jews would suffer something like a permanent state of pogrom, a fate more severe than loss of legal equality. But traditional Jewish optimism had confronted persecution many times before, and even now few Jews had come to believe that the Nazis could rule the world. Whether Jews put their faith in God, the Allies, or the Red Army, they still expected a rapid defeat of Hitler.

Within a few months, however, the Germans began to separate the Jews physically from the rest of the population. The ghettos and Star of David armbands came to symbolize a systematic program to wipe out European Jewry through hunger and sickness, and to exploit their labor and plunder their property. In Germany, holding on and holding out meant the struggle for rights. In the East European ghetto, the struggle was for life itself.

Still, the Jews of Europe rallied with energy, inventiveness,

174

von **18**^--**19**^- ein kleines
Schwätzchen

von **20**·**21**^- Sind wir
mit irdischen
Speisen beschäftigt

von **21**^--**22**^- Liebesgeflüster

von **22**^--**23**^- Die Hoch-
burg ruft

von **23**·**24**^- wir legen
uns zu
Bett.

VON **24**^--**7**^- Ruhe überall
nur die Ratten
treiben ihr Spiel.

and optimism to survive. Everywhere, intermediaries such as church and foreign government authorities were asked to bargain with the Germans; money was raised to ransom captives, and huge masses of Jews attempted illegal flight, inside Poland and out. Despite differences of opinion as to strategy, despite grossly insufficient resources, and despite even the occasional greed and selfishness of a minority of Jewish officials, the Jewish community in Europe and throughout the world pulled together with one goal in mind—to keep the Jews alive, to sustain them physically and morally. In this time of extreme crisis, the humane values of normal existence—protecting the family, educating the children, feeding the hungry, caring for the sick, satisfying cultural and intellectual needs—remained uppermost for the vast majority of Jews.

DEPORTATION

The third and final stage of the Jewish situation came with the deportations from the ghettos. The Jews realized that they now confronted a more severe threat to their existence than before, but few knew or expected they would die. The German strategy of lies and deceptions convinced many Jews that they were being resettled for hard labor, simply a form of persecution less familiar than the ghetto.

After information of mass shootings and gassing filtered into the ghettos, the first response everywhere was shocked disbelief. Even the unrestrained cruelties committed by the Germans until now had not prepared the Jews to grasp the facts of systematic mass murder. Closely guarded and unmercilessly terrorized, the Jews had no way of verifying the reports which came to them. No historical logic could suggest that the Germans would destroy even Jews working for war industries. The idea of annihilating innocent civilian men, women, and children in death camps was so incredible that even resistance fighters often failed to believe the threatening news they heard.

GUILT AND
INNOCENCE

One question reverberates through all accounts of the Holocaust—could lives have been saved? Did the Judenräte officials have opportunities or resources to prevent the Germans from carrying out the deportations, or at least to warn Jews not to submit? Did anyone really have enough information to devise strategies of survival?

Where tactical options existed and were tried, they hardly
ever worked. Refusal to cooperate usually resulted in being shot
immediately. Those who brought bribes or ransom to the Germans
often disappeared forever. Even rescue through work rarely succeeded
for very long. As is common in disasters, Jewish leaders tried to save as
many people as possible, but there were hardly enough lifeboats for
those on this sinking ship.

Those who survive disasters, natural or man-made, often feel guilty that they are living while so many others perished. This sense of guilt afflicted Jews who remained in the ghettos after the deportations, those who lived through the mass killings, and especially leaders who never knew for certain how they could save anyone. The powerlessness of the Jews who faced the Final Solution heightened their feelings of guilt, because Judaism placed upon each Jew the obligation for his or her own life and for the survival of the community. Zelig Kalmanovich (1881–1944), a scholar and writer, spoke for all when he wrote in his diary of the terrible dilemmas confronting the Jews in those days: "All are guilty, or perhaps more truly, all are innocent and holy."

---

**Reward and Punishment**  Since the beginning of recorded history, thinkers have wrestled with the problem of good and evil and their results. Are the righteous rewarded for their righteousness? Are the evil punished for the harm they inflict? The Bible states that God will reward those who follow His laws and punish those who turn aside to do evil (Deuteronomy 28; Psalms 92:8). The two daughter-religions of Judaism, Christianity and Islam, have traditionally taken this to mean that God will reward and punish people in the next life, if not in this world. But the rabbis pointed out that such rewards and punishments as the Bible speaks of could be found in the course of history as well (Sanhedrin 90a; Avot 2:7).

Unfortunately the events of history may also be read in a more tragic light. Often, as in the case of the Holocaust, the innocent suffer horribly. Of course the ancient rabbis pointed out that such innocent people would be rewarded by God in the life to come, but this explanation was insufficient even for their time and seems inadequate when applied to the mass murders of the innocent carried on by the Nazis.

The question of why the innocent suffer and why the righteous are put to death may very well be beyond our capacity to understand. But one more rabbinic footnote may be in order. Ultimately, the rabbis pointed out, the control of good and evil lies within each of us and we are rewarded or punished according to our own deeds. But we are not alone in the world. Each of us is a part of a generation which may be good or evil. In this sense, people often suffer unfairly because of the sins of others of their own generation (Ḥullin 142a).

Though it does not answer the question, it is nevertheless a fact that Hitler's plan of world domination was brought to a crushing halt by his own insistence that so much emphasis be placed upon the destruction of the Jewish people. Though he tried, even to the end, to cover up what he had done, the judgment of history is clear. The Germany he left behind was impoverished and ruined; the finest of its youth had been needlessly sacrificed on the field of battle; the glory of its culture ended in embarrassment and shame.

**Death** The Holocaust came to represent darkness, even as creation is symbolized by light (Genesis 1). We know, though we will never fully understand, that "all who have been born are destined to die" (Avot 4:22). This is the mystery of our limits, even as God is the mystery of infinity. The rabbis saw death as a time when we make the passage from this world to the next, when our souls which are holy leave our earthly shape which is dust. Death in Judaism is the final atonement before the final judgment; and our lives and all the things we have done must prepare us always to be ready for that moment as best we can. In a sense, the Holocaust is a record of death; in another sense, studying this record prepares us with a deeper understanding of life.

# DOCUMENTS OF THE HOLOCAUST

Without the benefits of freedom or security, the Jews of Nazi-occupied Europe were unable to keep records as massive and detailed as those of the government. Life had lost all sense of normalcy and stability, but the Judenräte, political parties, and many individual Jews were determined that some memory of their struggle should survive. They wrote down what they could, then hid these documents or gave them to non-Jewish friends. Perhaps the greatest effort of this kind was the *Oneg Shabbat* archive, directed by Emanuel Ringelblum in Warsaw. Hundreds of underground newspapers, private diaries, and transcribed interviews were preserved, and the Warsaw project set the example for similar ones in the Bialystok and Vilna ghettos. Even the inmates of Auschwitz managed to contribute to the preservation of history, by burying a significant number of memoirs which were later discovered.

---

1. As the web of Nazi persecution began slowly to encompass the Jews during the early 1930s, the Jewish communities of Europe were struck by a wave of hysteria and despair. Unprecedented numbers of Jews committed suicide during these terrible days, and though these represented but a fraction of one percent of the Jewish population, their deaths were an awful blow to the general morale. To fight against this "epidemic," rabbis and community leaders urged their fellow Jews to maintain hope.

COLOGNE PUBLIC APPEAL AGAINST SUICIDE (MID-1933)

Under the shattering impact of the events of recent weeks, during which suicide claimed victim upon victim within our community, we turn to you, men and women of the Jewish community, with the appeal:

*Maintain your courage and will to live, preserve your confidence in God and in yourself!*

The fate which has befallen each one of us is a part of the great universal Jewish suffering: Let us bear it together and help one another fraternally! Advisory boards of our Gemeinde as well as the homes of all members of the undersigned bodies are open to you — come to us with your spiritual and material needs; we will advise and help you as much as we can.

Do not take the path into darkness from which there is no return. Think of those whom you must leave behind in all their sorrow and affliction; think of human and Jewish destiny: do not lose hope for a better future!

2. As the Jews moved from freedom to ghettos, their struggle for faith intensified. If God cared for the people of Israel, why were they suffering so badly now? If the Germans were able to put their most evil designs into practice, where was the salvation and the justice which Judaism promised?

*O look from heaven and behold*
Look down from the skies and see!
*For we have become a derision,*
*A derision among the nations.*
We are surely a laughingstock to them.
*We are accounted as sheep to the slaughter.*
O Creator, how can You look upon this?
Indeed, we never were at ease,
We were always to the slaughter.

A SONG OF THE CHEŁMNO GHETTO (ITALICS INDICATES BIBLICAL QUOTATIONS)

Therefore we plead with You ever:
Help us now, Guardian of Israel,
Take notice now of our tears,
For still do we proclaim "Hear O Israel!"
O, take notice, Guardian of this nation.
Show all the people that You are our God,
We have indeed none other, just You alone,
Whose Name is One.

*Strangers say there is no salvation.*
The nations say that for us
There is no hope.
We may be driven,
We may be tormented.
We have no one to whom
We can complain.
But we surely know
That You are in heaven!
Of You the Bible says:

*He doth neither slumber nor sleep.*
You must surely protect
Your children.
Therefore we know
That You are in heaven —
With miracles and wonders.

181

*Spare us O Lord,*
*Surrender us not to their hand.*
Have pity, do not yield us
Into their hands.
*Wherefore should the nations say:*
*'Where is their God?'*
That is always their cry.
O my Jews, my Jews, what are you doing here?
Gather your packs and take ye to Zion!
We would have fled
But the way is not open.
Why do You let them treat us thus?

---

3. The young people of the ghettos would not stand passively in the face of German persecution. The starving needed food, and the laws of the Germans could certainly be overlooked in order to save lives. Despite great risks, smuggling became a profession commonly practiced, especially by the young.

HENRYKA
LAZAWERT:
"THE LITTLE
SMUGGLER"

Over the wall, through holes, and past the guard,
Through the wires, ruins, and fences,
Plucky, hungry, and determined
I sneak through, dart like a cat.

At noon, at night, at dawn,
In snowstorm, cold or heat,
A hundred times I risk my life
And put my head on the line.

Under my arm a gunny sack,
Tatters on my back,
On nimble young feet,
With endless fear in my heart.

But one must endure it all,
One must bear it all,
So that tomorrow morning
The fine folk can eat their fill.

Over the wall, through holes and bricks,
At night, at dawn, at noon,
Plucky, hungry, artful,
I move silently like a shadow.

And if the hand of destiny

Should seize me in the game,
That's a common trick of life.
You, mother, do not wait up for me.

> I will return no more to you,
> My voice will not be heard from afar.
> The dust of the street will bury
> The lost fate of a child.

> And only one request
> Will stiffen on my lips:
> Who, mother mine, who
> Will bring your bread tomorrow?

---

4. The leaders of ghetto Jewry confronted insurmountable problems, but most struggled valiantly to keep spirits up and heads clear. Which tactics would prove most effective, or at least would do the least harm? The community was so adrift from normal, predictable life that few officials could act confidently in the face of constant fear and uncertainty.

Many people are complaining because I arrange plays for children, festive openings of nurseries with orchestras playing, etc. I am reminded of a movie: a sinking ship—the captain orders the jazz band to play to lift the passengers' spirits. I have decided to imitate this captain.

A JUDENRAT LEADER'S DIARY ENTRY (JULY 8, 1942)

---

5. Soon enough, the deportations began, Now everyone, and particularly the Judenrat leaders, was living in the shadow of death. Who could be saved, who spared—if only for a while? Would these days of unbearable anguish come to an end, or were they the final chapter for European Jewry?

'. . . Perhaps this plan is devilish, perhaps not, but I cannot hold back from uttering it: "Give me these sick and in their place we can rescue the healthy." I know how dearly each family, especially among Jews, cherishes its sick. But with such an edict, we have to weigh and measure: Who should, can, and may be saved? Common sense dictates that we should save those capable of being saved, those who have prospects of survival, and not those who can't be saved anyway.

JOSEF ZELKOWICZ: "DAYS OF NIGHTMARE" (THE LODZ JUDENRAT CHAIRMAN'S SPEECH, FRIDAY, SEPTEMBER 4, 1942)

'We live, after all, in the ghetto. Our life is so austere that we don't even have enough for the healthy, much less for the sick. Each of us keeps the sick man alive at the price of our own health. We give the sick man our bread. We give him our bit of sugar, our piece of meat, and the consequence is that not only does the sick man not become well, but we become sick. Naturally, such sacrifices are noble. But at a time when we must choose either to sacrifice the sick man, who not only has no chance of becoming well but is even likely to make others sick, or to rescue a well man. I could not mull over this problem for long, and I was forced to decide in favor of the well man. I have therefore given orders to the doctors and they will be compelled to turn over all the incurably ill in order to rescue in their stead all those who are well and who want, and are able, to live.' (Terrible weeping.)

'I understand you, mothers, I see your tears. I can also feel your hearts, fathers, who, tomorrow, after your children have been taken from you, will be going to work, when just yesterday you had been playing with your dear little children. I know all this and I sympathize with it. Since 4 P.M. yesterday, upon hearing the decree, I have utterly collapsed. I live with your grief, and your sorrow torments me, and I don't know how and with what strength I can live through it. I must tell you a secret. They demanded twenty-four thousand victims, three thousand persons a day, for eight days, but I succeeded in getting them to reduce the number to twenty thousand, and perhaps even fewer than twenty thousand, but only on condition that these will be children to the age of ten. Children over ten are safe. Since children and old people add up only to thirteen thousand, we will have to meet the quota by adding the sick as well.

'It is hard for me to speak. I have no strength. I will only utter the appeal I make to you: Help me carry out the action! I tremble. I am frightened at the thought that others, God forbid, might take it into their own hands.

'You see before you a broken man. Don't envy me. This is the most difficult order that I have ever had to carry out. I extend to you failing and trembling hands and I beg you: Give into my hands the victims, thereby to ensure against further victims, thereby to protect a community of a hundred thousand Jews.' . . .

---

6. Confusion and despair soon spilled over into anger. The last Jews to die in the Holocaust would not surrender their lives to the Nazis without resisting with every ounce of strength at their command. The heroic leaders of the last stand in the Warsaw ghetto urged all who still survived to struggle through their final days with courage, and conscience, and with pride.

Jews, citizens of the Warsaw ghetto, be alert, do not believe a single word or act of the SS bandits. Deathly danger threatens. Remember the last "action"—seizing Jews to send them "for work" to Lublin. They needed "tailors," but seized old people, children. People were seized for "work," and taken away just as they were, in their bare rags. The old story repeats itself once again: messages arrive and letters saying that they were indeed sent to Lublin. We remind you of the "letters," the "reliable" messages from Brest-Livtos, Minsk, Bialystok, which the Germans fabricated. We remind you that Belżec is located in the Lublin district, where tens of thousands of Jews have been murdered according to the Treblinka method.

Let's not fool ourselves.

The Lublin "action" of November 10 and 11 teaches us also something else.

Once more the Germans have found helpers and agents among the Jews themselves. Once again they have found scoundrels who have, with their own hands, delivered their brothers to the slaughter, the price for saving their own vile, despicable lives. The gangrene which the Jewish police and Judenrat members has let loose in Warsaw has infected the circles of the workshop managements, often run by the meanest scoundrels, ready for any infamy.

Do not believe the Jewish "big wheels," the directors of the workshops, the foremen—they are your enemies. Do not let yourselves be fooled by them.

Do not delude yourselves, and do not let yourselves be deluded, that the better craftsmen, the senior workers who have numbered tickets, are safe, and so let the weaker ones, the unprotected be delivered [to the Germans].

All are endangered.

Let nobody dare lend a hand, nor help—actively or passively—to deliver into the hands of the executioner his brother, his comrade, his neighbor, or his coworker.

Let us not act like scum, like vermin, in the face of destruction. Help one another.

The vile traitors who help the enemy must be spewed out of our camp.

Do not let yourselves be destroyed like sheep.

Prepare yourselves to defend your lives.

Remember that also you—the civilian Jewish population—are at the front in the fight for freedom and humanity.

The enemy has already been severely hurt. Let us bravely

and nobly defend our honor.

Long live freedom!

---

7. The cries of Europe's Jews went unanswered, and their centuries-old and renowned community succumbed unmercifully to the weapons of the enemy. Across the seas, Jews in other lands survived, but none would easily muster the courage of those who perished in the modern world's most tragic time.

FROM ZELIG KALMANOVICH'S DIARY (DECEMBER 27, 1942)

Eventually the Jewish people itself will forget this branch that was broken off. It will have to do without it. From the healthy trunk will come forth branches and blossoms and leaves. There is still strength and life. Dried up and decayed—this happens to every tree. There are still thousands of years ahead. Lamentation for the dead, of course, that is natural, particularly if they are your own, close to you. But the Jewish people must not be confused. The mourning for close ones— some people bear their sorrow long; most find comfort. Human nature—such is the world. Whatever the earth covers up is forgotten. In the ghetto itself we see how people forget. It cannot be otherwise. It certainly is not wrong. The real motive in mourning is after all fear of one's own end. Wherein are we better than those tens of thousands? It must happen to us, too. If we only had a guarantee of survival! But that does not exist and one cannot always be fearful, then the feeling of fear is projected into mourning for the fallen, and sorrow over the destruction of Jewry. Spare yourself the sorrow! The Jewish people will not be hurt. It will, it is to be hoped, emerge fortified by the trial. This should fill the heart with joyous gratitude to the sovereign of history.

# SOME DATES TO REMEMBER

| | |
|---|---|
| **1889** | Hitler born |
| **1905** | First Russian publication of the *Protocols of the Elders of Zion* |
| **Nov. 11, 1918** | End of World War I |
| **1920** | Hitler made *Fuehrer* of the Nazi party |
| **1925** | *Mein Kampf* published |
| **Jan. 30, 1933** | Nazi accession to power. Hitler appointed Chancellor of the Reich |
| **April 1, 1933** | Beginning of Nazi boycott against Jewish businesses |
| **Sept. 15, 1935** | Nuremburg Laws drive Jews from public and professional life |
| **Nov. 9, 1938** | "Night of Shattered Glass" |
| **May 17, 1939** | British White Paper restricts immigration to Palestine |
| **Aug. 23, 1939** | Nazi-Soviet pact signed |
| **Sept. 1, 1939** | German invasion of Poland begins World War II |
| **Sept. 3, 1939** | Britain and France declare war against Germany |
| **Nov., 1940** | Establishment of the Warsaw ghetto |
| **June 22, 1941** | German invasion of Russia |
| **Sept. 1941** | Mass murder of Jews at Babi Yar |
| **Oct. 1, 1941** | Jewish emigration from Nazi-occupied Europe halted |
| **Dec. 7, 1941** | Japanese attack Pearl Harbor, Hawaii |
| **Dec. 8, 1941** | United States and Great Britain declare war against Japan |
| **Dec. 11, 1941** | United States declares war against Germany |
| **March 1942** | Mass extermination camps begin to operate |
| **Dec. 17, 1942** | Allied condemnation of Nazi extermination program |
| **April 19, 1943** | Nazis begin to attack the Warsaw ghetto |

| | |
|---|---|
| **June 6, 1944** | Allied landing at Normandy, France |
| **April 30, 1945** | Hitler commits suicide |
| **May 8, 1945** | Surrender of Germany to the Allies |
| **June 26, 1945** | United Nations established |
| **1945-1946** | International Military Tribunal war crimes trials in Nuremburg |
| **May 14, 1948** | Establishment of the State of Israel |
| **1961-1962** | Trial and execution of Adolf Eichmann |

# INDEX